Images of
HUDDERSFIELD

Images of
HUDDERSFIELD

The Huddersfield Daily
Examiner

Kirklees
METROPOLITAN · COUNCIL
CULTURAL SERVICES

Breedon Books
Publishing Company
Derby

First published in Great Britain by
The Breedon Books Publishing Company Limited
44 Friar Gate, Derby, DE1 1DA.
1994

ISBN 1 873626 92 4

Printed and bound by Butler & Tanner, Frome and London.
Covers printed by BDC Printing Services Limited of Derby

Contents

The Kirklees Photographic Archive

Kirklees Cultural Services, Museums and Arts section hold, with a deposit agreement, the *Huddersfield Daily Examiner* collection of negatives. These date from 1946 to the early 1980s and contain many of the photographs which appeared in the *Examiner* during these years.

In addition, the archive also contains a number of earlier collections acquired originally by individual museums now in Kirklees. These date from 1865 onwards and represent the work of both amateur and professional photographers. Within these collections images exist for every area of Huddersfield and many parts of Britain and Europe.

How to order copies of photographs

Copies of many of the photographs in this book can be purchased from the Photographic Archive which is based at the Tolson Museum, Ravensknowle Park, Wakefield Road, Huddersfield, HD5 8DJ, Tel (0484) 530591. Simple or very specific enquiries can usually be dealt with by telephone but for more general searches it may be necessary to visit the archive for which an appointment is essential.

Acknowledgements

Many people have helped in the preparation of this book. Special mention must be made to Katrina Ward of the Photographic Archive for her help and guidance through the collection. To the staff of Huddersfield Local History Library and Stock Management at Cultural Services HQ while the photographs were being researched. Robert Drummond and Andrew Flynn of the *Examiner* for their enthusiasm and help, especially in asking *Examiner* readers to provide information on some of the photographs for which there were few details, and, of course, the readers themselves who rang in with the answers. A personal thanks must be given to my father-in-law, G.R.Schofield, whose own photographs have been included, and to my husband Colin for their encouragement and local knowledge that has added so much interest to my work.

Isobel Schofield
Huddersfield
July 1994

Introduction

HUDDERSFIELD sits in the valley at the confluence of the rivers Holme and Colne. An industrial town, its inhabitants were described by John Wesley in 1757 as 'a wilder people I never saw in England'. Many changes during the later eighteenth and nineteenth centuries resulted in the town being described by F.Engles as 'the handsomest by far of the factory towns in Yorkshire and Lancashire' (F.Engles, *The Condition of the Working Class in England* [1848]).

Drawings and prints recorded the appearance of an area, but the development of photography meant that a specific moment could be captured for ever. Over the years photographs have been taken by individuals and professionals. Huddersfield is lucky to have a Photographic Archive that includes early photographs of the town and surrounding area and photographs taken by the *Huddersfield Daily Examiner.*

The collection deposited with Kirklees by the *Examiner* dates from 1946. In the preparation of this book, a deliberate decision was made to use a majority of photographs from the late 1940s and early 1950s, recording life in the area before the rapid changes of the 1960s. A large proportion of the photographs were taken to illustrate a news story and, wherever possible, this story has been briefly retold.

We have endeavoured to reflect as many aspects of Huddersfield and its surrounding areas as possible. There are so many good and interesting photographs available that shortage of space means that some villages or specific memories have been omitted.

The arrangement of the photographs is deliberate in that they start in the Town Centre, move out to circle the districts of the County Borough and then to the outlying villages and hamlets. A selection of photographs on agriculture and industry of the area moves on to transport, disasters, medicine, education, culture including music and the theatre. Sport is followed by special events such as Royal visits, and finally a reflection of the some of the annual events that take place specifically in this area.

We hope that these photographs will recall many happy memories of times gone by, that parents and grandparents will talk to their children of their own childhood so that we do not lose all that it meant to be born a Yorkshire 'cock' or 'rose' in the Huddersfield area.

Abbreviations
Ex *Huddersfield Daily Examiner*
KCS Kirklees Cultural Services
GRS G. Raymond Schofield

Huddersfield Town Centre

View of Huddersfield from Longley, 1837 painted by G.D.Tomlinson. (*KCS*)

'Sun Kissed Huddersfield' photographed from Castle Hill in August 1959. The Fanny Moor estate in Lowerhouses is in the foreground. (*Ex 2654-59*)

Huddersfield by night in 1950, Lowerhouses is in the foreground. (*GRS*)

View across Huddersfield from Kilner Bank looking towards Castle Hill in August 1948. (*Ex 4464-48*)

St Peter's Parish Church tower was in urgent need of restoration in 1953 and was hidden by scaffolding for several months. The *Examiner* took advantage of the scaffolding to take the following three photographs.

Cross Church Street looking towards St Paul's Church with Castle Hill in the distance. (*Ex 4915-53*)

Kilner Bank showing the recently demolished area that is now the site of the Sports Centre, Crown House and the Telephone Exchange. (*Ex 4913-53*)

Lord Street towards the Leeds Road area with the cooling towers of the power station in the distance. *(Ex 4918-53)*

Huddersfield Market Place at the turn of the century. The water fountain, given to the town in 1888 by Sir John W.Ramsden, Bart., was later moved to Greenhead Park. *(0054/1444)*

Huddersfield Market Place and New Street in 1940. The Market Cross, dating from 1671, is the oldest structure in the town centre. (*KCS*)

Coronation decorations looking from John William Street to New Street, May 1953. (*Ex 2360-53*)

This zebra crossing on the corner of John William Street and Kirkgate was used to highlight the importance of road safety during National Pedestrian Crossing Week in April 1949. A gentleman's suit cost fifty shillings (£2.50) at Burton's, the tailors, hence the name 'The Fifty Shilling Tailors'. (*Ex 6570-49*)

In 1881 the Huddersfield Banking Company was responsible for the erection of this fine Italianate building on the corner of Cloth Hall Street. In 1971 the Midland Bank commissioned Peter Womersley to design and build its replacement. (*RH5/67*)

'Reflections in the rain, a sudden downpour converts New Street by night into fairyland' in November 1951. (*Ex 51-4016*)

Buxton Road in the 1960s. The West Riding and Curzon cinema were among the buildings demolished and replaced with C & A's and other retailers now on New Street. (*KCS*)

The Huddersfield Co-operative Society on Buxton Road pictured in the 1960s from the roundabout at the top of Chapel Hill. Built in several stages the main block dates from the late nineteenth century, and the newer section, dating from 1936, is described in *The Buildings of Huddersfield* by David Wyles 'as the best early example of a truly modern building in the town centre'. (*KCS*)

Kirkgate from the corner of New Street provided a bustling scene for the *Examiner* photographer in July 1955. (*Ex 3414-55*)

These old buildings at the corner of Lower Head Row and Beast Market were photographed in 1880. They were pulled down in 1897. *(0054/338)*

Harry Conroy (of Colne Bridge) is pictured receiving a sack of potatoes from Kenneth Hey (of Kirkheaton) outside the Wholesale Fruit and Vegetable Market in January 1957. The market buildings were restored in 1980 and now house the open markets. *(Ex 121-57)*

Byram Street from Packhorse Yard taken in the snow on 3 January 1949. (*Ex 5565-49*)

The junction of King Street with New Street taken in the early 1900s. (*KCS*)

The interior of the Huddersfield Market Hall in 1953. Demolished in 1970, the old Market Hall was replaced by the Queensgate Market on the Piazza. (*Ex 5090-53*)

This picture was taken from a window in Huddersfield Library which looked out over the rear of the Market Hall, Shambles and the Unicorn public house. Taken in October 1953 the Shambles had been in the news a few weeks previously when the traders were concerned that a ban on motor traffic on Shambles Lane and Victoria Lane, coupled with the shortage of storage space in the Market Hall would cause delivery problems. (*Ex 4861-53*)

Ramsden Street in June 1953 with the Library, the *Examiner* Offices and Borough Club decorated to celebrate the Coronation of Queen Elizabeth II. (*Ex 2363-53*)

The lower part of Ramsden Street was demolished to make way for the Piazza. Council offices were on the left with the Picture House and Ramsden Street Baths on the right. The coach was being towed from the Fire Station. (*Ex 4436A-48*)

Queen Street Mission was opened in 1880. In the *Census of Religious Worship* it was recorded that 777 adults attended the morning service on Mothering Sunday 1851. (*KCS*)

Queen Street Methodist Chapel photographed in 1954. The congregation moved to King Street Mission in 1970. A variety of uses for the building followed and it reopened in 1994 as the Lawrence Batley Theatre. (*Ex 271-54*)

Huddersfield Police Station on Peel Street was replaced by a new building on Albion Street. This site now houses the Queensgate Market built in the 1960s. (*KCS*)

Three of the 'powerful' Police patrol cars of 1948 were fitted with radios in June. People were asked to report anything suspicious from one of the 47 Police Boxes, private telephone or public boxes. (*Ex 3886-48*)

Watched by Sergeant Redfern, PC Taylor signs in at the Huddersfield Borough Police Station in December 1953. It was reported in 1952 that there were 169 men and six women to police a population of 130,000. (*Ex 5361-53*)

The last fire engines leave Princess Street in February 1961 making their way to their new home on Outcote Bank. (*Ex 466-61*)

New Gas showrooms were opened on the High Street in 1958. Ten years earlier the Huddersfield Corporation Gas showroom was on Byram Street and can be seen in the photograph of the Remembrance Day parade on page 184. (*Ex 4099-58*)

The Norwich Union Building at the corner of High Street and Market Street was the home of the Examiner Stationers opened in 1961.
(*Ex 3048-61*)

The Electricity Showrooms and Service Centre on Market Street in February 1954. Before the setting up of the British Electrical
Authority in 1948, the generation of electricity locally was controlled by the Huddersfield Corporation Electricity Committee. (*Ex 467-54*)

Imperial Arcade in 'Gala Dress' celebrated the Coronation of Queen Elizabeth II in this photograph taken on 13 May 1953. (*Ex 2036-53*)

The Huddersfield Cloth Hall, photographed in the 1920s, was erected in 1766 by Sir John Ramsden. It had become redundant by the mid-nineteenth century when cloth merchants started to conduct business from their own warehouses in the town centre. The Cloth Hall was demolished in 1930 and replaced by a cinema, and more recently by a row of shops. (*0054/218*)

The Estate Buildings in Westgate in around 1880. Built in 1871-72 by W.H.Crossland to house the Ramsden estate offices. (*RH6/4B*)

The corner of Westgate and Market Street in 1914. The awning probably covers the shop which had become Newby's fishmongers by the 'National Herring Week' featured in the next photograph. (*KCS*)

Newby's of Westgate entered this special display in a competition during National Herring Week in September 1951 and won the second prize of a display stand and £3 2s. 0d. (£3.10). The photograph shows from left to right Mr Tom Connelly (of Primrose Hill), ?, Betty Sykes (the cashier), Winnie ?, ?, and the manager Mr Ted Addison (with a moustache). (*Ex 3079-51*)

A police search for intruders on 27 August 1948 closed off Byram Arcade for 7 hours. The burglar alarm at Rushworth's had gone off, but before the entire block was sealed off the intruders escaped. However a suspect was later arrested. (*Ex 4583-48*)

St George's Square is graced by the elegant Huddersfield railway station designed by J.P. Pritchett and built in the late 1840s. The Square has been altered many times over the years. This photograph shows it in October 1947. (*Ex 2202-47*)

The statue of Robert Peel is reputed to have given offence to visiting royalty because it had its back to them as they left the station. The badly weathered statue was removed from St George's Square on 31 October 1949 and the base re-erected in Ravensknowle Park. (*Ex 9301-49*)

The lion on top of Lion Buildings has become one of the symbols of Huddersfield. According to legend, when the station clock strikes 13 times the lion comes down from the roof to walk around the square. It was repainted in 1948 by a team of painters from Kendall's in Byram Street led by Mr William Hartley and included, in a white boiler suit, Tom Bailey. The lion has since been replaced by a fibre glass copy. (*Ex 4519-48*)

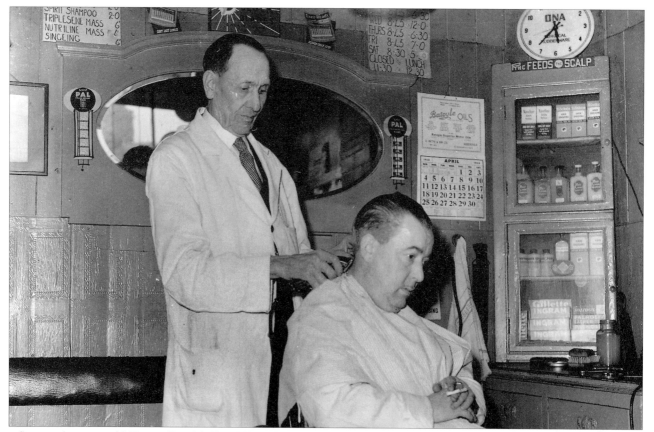

Seventy-three-year-old Thomas Brook believed himself to be the 'oldest' hairdresser in Huddersfield. After training in Bradford he owned a saloon in Sheepridge for 32 years but worked at weekends for Mr H.Shaw at his saloon in Viaduct Street when he was photographed by the *Examiner* on 22 April 1954. (*Ex 2022-54*)

Shops in Northgate and Northumberland Street were reprieved by the Ministry of Transport and Civil Aviation in April 1959. They were not needed as part of the redevelopment of the junction of Leeds Road with Southgate and the ring road. (*Ex 1342-59*)

Castlegate was regularly used as an overnight 'tank park' in 1953. The tanks were in transit from Royal Ordnance Fenton in Leeds. The *Examiner* reported that David Griffiths MP queried their safety in the Houses of Commons. (*Ex 1946-53*)

Plans were published in December 1951 to close Princess Street by the erection of 'temporary' buildings by the Huddersfield Technical College. The 'temporary' buildings cost around £8,000 and were still there in 1994. (*Ex 4242-51*)

The junction of Southgate, Ramsden Street and Wakefield Road at Shore Head has altered greatly since this photograph was taken in 1955. (*Ex 572-55*)

Around the Districts of the County Borough

A Victorian cabriolet trundles along Wakefield Road at Aspley in 1953. Driven by John Atkinson, the *Examiner* reported that the owner, Mr Sam S.Kaye, had bought it from 'a large Scottish estate' and wondered if the cabriolet had carried Queen Victoria. *(Ex 2187-53)*

Kilner Bank from Wakefield Road, Moldgreen in March 1953. *(Ex 1175-53)*

Moldgreen Congregational Church and the Regal cinema on Wakefield Road, Moldgreen in June 1954. Both buildings were demolished in the 1980s as part of the road widening scheme. (*Ex 3227-54*)

Mrs Birtles retired in November 1950 from Moldgreen Post Office after 22 years service. During her time the work had increased eightfold. (*Ex 13913A-50*)

Spring in Ravensknowle Park as crocuses bloom in front of the Cloth Hall Clock Tower in 1954. (*Ex 1426-54*)

The post-war housing crisis resulted in the building of these Pre-fabs. In 1951 the winner of the 'Best kept Corporation House Garden' was in Dalton. (*Ex 3122-51*)

In December 1946 there were 5,000 people on the waiting list for a council house. In 1951 these 'Steel framed houses' in Dalton, were reported as being 'much quicker to put up', with the roof going 'on after the framework is up'. The buildings were of a traditional appearance. (*Ex 3544-51*)

Cottages on Northgate in Almondbury were about to be demolished when this photograph was taken in June 1952. They were replaced by a shopping arcade a few years later. (*Ex 2371-52*)

Wormall Hall in Almondbury dates from around 1400. In 1631 the lower part was encased in stone by Isaac Wormall whose initials I.W. and M. for his wife Mary appear with the date carved on the lintel above the door. In 1948, Westgate still retained its rural charm. (*Ex 4490-48*)

Dr W.J. Varley carried out excavations on Castle Hill in 1939, from 1946-47 and between 1969 and 1973. In August 1948 the research team excavated the foundations of what they believed to be a dungeon with a Norman arch. (*Ex 4580-48*)

'Study in sunshine and shadow', Robin Hood Hill at Berry Brow in July 1948. (*Ex 4170-48*)

Newsome Mills in 1953. (*Ex 1174-53*)

Paper recycling is not new – for many years during and after the World War Two everyone was encouraged to 'save waste paper'. In this picture, taken in March 1956, salvage is being collected in Towngate, Newsome by Norman Ellis (with rake) and his colleague.
(*Ex 1279-56*)

Taylor Hill and Newsome as seen from Hanson Lane, Lockwood in August 1947. (*Ex 1929-47*)

Described by the *Examiner* in May 1953 as 'once of rural charm, with the promise of a spa'. Lockwood Scar was taken over by the industrial revolution. (*Ex 2032-53*)

Chapel Hill looking up towards the Huddersfield Co-operative Society in 1946. (*Ex 180-46*)

This part of Huddersfield disappeared in 1961 to make way for the 'new' ring road. Chapel Hill is on the right-hand side looking down. (*Ex 161-61*)

Albert Street, Lockwood is deserted as the mill workers celebrate the new year of 1947. (*Ex 373-47*)

The centre of Lockwood was one of the busiest corners in the locality and at times was 'one of the most awkward' when this photograph was taken in 1953. Still a problem corner, this view of Lockwood Bar from Meltham Road shows Bridge Street (on the right) leading to Woodhead Road, ahead is the road to the town centre, and Swan Lane is on the left. (*Ex 1697-53*)

'February Reflections', Beaumont Park Lake in February 1951. (*Ex 496-51*)

Meltham Road, Netherton, photographed in June 1954, was noted for its lamp-post 'island' in front of the Post Office. The lamp-post was later moved after it had been hit by a lorry. (*Ex 3307-54*)

Harry Taylor and Leslie Leach are pictured in 1953 awaiting a 'Ghost Train' on Netherton Station – no passenger trains had run since 1949. (*Ex 1665-56*)

A 'healthy hill top suburb' of over 270 houses and bungalows was reported to be shooting up at Crosland Moor in the summer of 1954. (*Ex 2807-54*)

Hardware shop run by Mr T.Sadd, a general dealer, in Crosland Moor taken on 2 May 1956. (*Ex 1902-56*)

Oldfield Square at Thornton Lodge was photographed in October 1952. Built into the sides of the houses were 'motto stones'. On one
of them the Sportsman's Lodge was written:
No more fellow soldiers
Thy sword shall I wield
Like a warrior I've fought
Like a winner I'll yield.
1831
(*Ex 4365-52*)

The Colne Valley photographed in 1957. Milnsbridge viaduct in the centre, Salendine Nook and Oakes on the horizon. (*Ex 2452-57*)

The Whit Monday procession on Manchester Road left Milnsbridge Parish Church on its way to the Jubilee Fields on 3 June 1950. The May Queen (Carol Greenfield) and her retinue followed the Kirkburton Victoria band. The vicar Revd G.A.Saxton and the church choir sang hymns at various points along the route. (*Ex 11670-50*)

Paddock Head in September 1951. (*Ex 3347-51*)

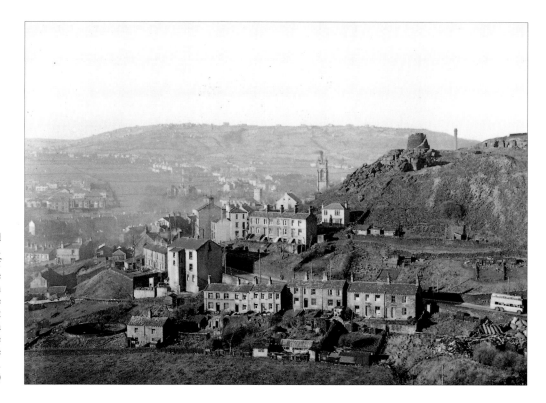

Nab Tower and Longwood in 1956. Although a variety of legends explain the origin of the tower in the early years of the nineteenth century, it rapidly became a meeting point and the home of the 'Longwood Sing'. (*Ex 4789-56*)

Outlane in the grip of winter in December 1951. Twenty years later the M62, opened by Queen Elizabeth II on 14 October 1971, cut the village in half. (*Ex 4313-51*)

The Nags Head, Lindley Moor was in sunshine while the rest of the town suffered from the 'worst' fogs for many years in November 1948. (*Ex 5319-48*)

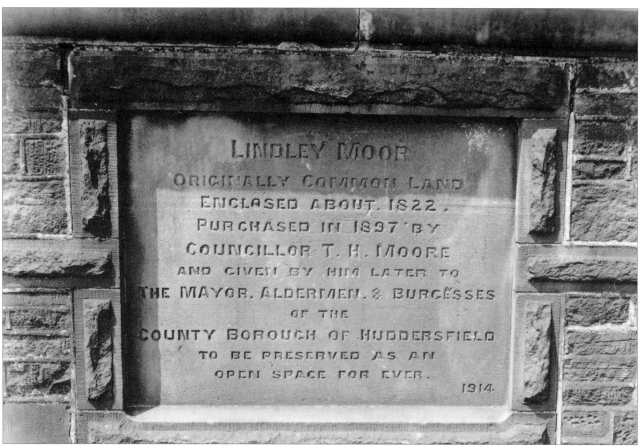

This plaque celebrating the purchase of Lindley Moor 'to be preserved as an open space for ever' was erected in 1952. In 1994 the residents of Lindley were fighting plans to build an industrial estate on nearby farmland. (*Ex 2395-52*)

Morris Bower was for many years Huddersfield's own weatherman. Working at the Oakes Meteorological Station as a member of the Survey of Thunderstorm in the British Isles he also prepared reports for radio and television. He is pictured showing the Stevenson Screen, used to protect the meteorological instruments, to two young visitors in 1956. (*Ex 229-56*)

Lindley Zion Methodist Church celebrated 150 years of witness in 1947. Originally founded in 1797 when members formed a New Connexion meeting in Lidget Fold. (*Ex 2335-47*)

Lindley Clock Tower, built in 1899, was commissioned by James Neild Sykes, uncle of the Art Nouveau architect Edgar Wood who also designed Banney Royd. The distinctive sculptures are by Sterling Lee. (*KCS*)

Quarmby Old Hall in September 1953 was one of the many old halls which have survived in the Huddersfield area. (*Ex 4227-53*)

The lake in Greenhead Park in 1900. Later drained, it is now an area of grass and flower beds. One of the shelters has been demolished and replaced by an alpine garden. (*KCS*)

'Autumn comes to Greenhead Park' was the heading used by the *Examiner* as they recorded this idyllic scene in September 1952. The Cenotaph was erected in 1924, and rededicated in May 1947 to include casualties from the World War Two. (*Ex 4820-52*)

Highfield Chapel, built in 1772, was the first Independent church founded in the town. This chapel was replaced in 1844 by a larger building, which in turn was converted to apartments in the early 1990s. The Sunday School run by Church members, founded in 1811, was one of the first to offer free education to children too poor to attend a day school in the town. (*KCS*)

Banney Royd, built for William H. Armitage at the turn of the century, is a Grade I listed building. The house was bought in 1918 for £12,500 by Lt. Col. Sir Emmanuel Hoyle who commissioned a series of photographs of the house in 1919 of which two are printed here. (*KCS*)

Banney Royd drawing room in 1919. At that time it was a private house but was requisitioned during the World War Two and has had a number of uses since. The most recent being as Kirklees Teachers' Centre. (*KCS*)

Birkby from Highfields, photographed in May 1951, with the spire of St John's Church in the foreground and Cowcliffe on the horizon. (*Ex 1472-51*)

The Old Bay Hall in Birkby was occupied by a tanner named John Brook in the 1560s. This photograph was taken on 5 November 1953. (*Ex 4944-53*)

Residents of Pollard Street in Fartown were told that this air raid shelter could not be demolished in 1958. The Council could not do anything to help – it was owned by the Home Office, whose policy was to 'build up Civil Defence resources'. (*Ex 2647-58*)

On 9 July 1949 it was reported in the *Examiner* that £1,500 had been stolen from Hillhouse PO. The safe keys were stolen – along with trousers – while Tom Hallawell the Sub-Postmaster was asleep. (*Ex 7724-49*)

The new crematorium in Fixby was reported as 'almost ready' in March 1958. Built at a cost of £103,000 it was opened on 15 April. (*Ex 923-58*)

This butcher's shop in Brackenhall was photographed in 1954. (*Ex 3500-54*)

'Double-decker' houses at Colne Bridge on the outskirts of Huddersfield in June 1953. (*Ex 2854-53*)

Featured in the *Examiner* during June 1953, this house, built in 1751, was one of the oldest houses in Bradley. The house was formerly a well known coaching inn – the Golden Cock. (*Ex 2833-53*)

St Thomas's church at Bradley. Photographed in June 1951 the train is rushing through the site of the 'recently demolished' Bradley Station. (*Ex 2762-53*)

'Reed fringed canal and ruined mill' shows the history of water transport as the canal winds through Deighton towards the Calder Valley in June 1951. (*Ex 1990-51*)

Photographed in 1953, the Huddersfield Open Market was held on Ray Street, behind the bus depot on Leeds Road. The market was relocated in the 1970s to the Victorian fruit and vegetable market on Byram Street. (*Ex 5197-53*)

Ray Street Market looking towards the bus depot in April 1961. (*Ex 1398-61*)

The Wider Circle - Villages of Hill and Valley

Kirkheaton Parish Church had been destroyed by fire in 1886, only the fifteenth century tower and Black Dick's tomb survived.(*Ex 1154-47*)

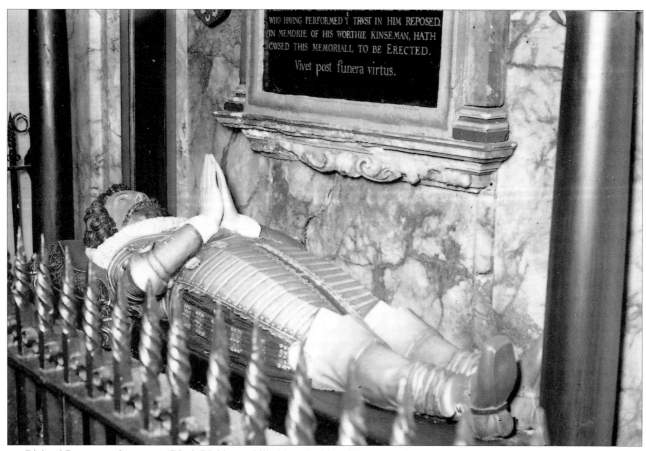

Richard Beaumont, known as 'Black Dick', was killed in a duel in 1631. Reputed to have been a highway robber, he was being blackmailed by his opponent. Gambling debts resulted in the sale of the estate to his uncle, William Ramsden, one of the family that was to own most of Huddersfield. Black Dick's ghost was reported to walk at midnight – but had not been seen for some time when these photographs were taken in May 1947. (*Ex 1157-47*)

PC Patrick E.Turney patrols his beat through the centre of Flockton village in January 1957. (*Ex 489-57*)

Emley Cross, photographed in 1953, had been whitewashed annually by the Parker family for over 150 years. According to legend, a woman in a halter was once sold at the cross. (*Ex 1463-53*)

The village of Emley in the snow of 1955. (*Ex 188-55*)

The Drapery branch of the Scissett Industrial and Co-operative Society in Clayton West was photographed as part of a feature on the village and its people. Mrs N.Green is seen showing a garment to Mrs M.Brown. (*Ex 5476-56*)

Scissett from Bagden Wood in 1953. (*Ex 4980-53*)

This old farm in the village of Scissett was photographed in November 1953. (*Ex 4981-53*)

'A pretty corner'. The road to Emley, along which two miners are returning from work, shows the important part coal mining still played in Skelmanthorpe in July 1953. (*Ex 3357-53*)

Miss Maureen Sowerby at work in the local Co-operative Society in Skelmanthorpe. She had been chosen as 'Miss Denby Dale' just before this picture was taken in July 1953. (*Ex 3355-53*)

'Only gently touched by time', Kirkburton was mentioned in the Doomsday Book. Pictured in May 1953 the main road winds through the village. (*Ex 1934-53*)

'Special buses take children to secondary school' from Kirkburton in May 1953. (*Ex 1930-53*)

'Unchanged hamlet of Highburton in Kirkburton Urban District Council. The hamlet commands views over the valley of Fenay Beck'. Town Gate in June 1952. (*Ex 2184-52*)

According to tradition, Oliver Cromwell rested at the foot of the cross at Highburton, and it is now known as 'Cromwell's Seat'. The shaft is modern but the date of the cross is unknown. (*Ex 2006-53*)

Cumberworth Parish Church in August 1956. (*Ex 3780-56*)

The road winds through this idyllic view of Thunderbridge in the summer of 1947. (*Ex 1175-47*)

The village of Denby Dale, seen from Miller Hill in July 1954, is noted for producing the largest pies in the world. (*Ex 3639-54*)

The people of Denby Dale had hoped to bake a Coronation Pie in 1953 but were unable to because of meat rationing. However they were successful in September 1964 when it was paraded through the village on its way to Norman Park. The funds raised were used to build the Pie Hall and the huge pie dish became a raised flower bed in the car park. (*Ex 3551-64*)

The centre of Shepley in 1952. The village was noted for its tailors who used to live and work there but the trade was dying out by the 1950s. (*Ex 2867-52*)

The Junction Inn on the Shepley – New Mill Road in March 1953. In 1994 the pub was known as the Crossroads Inn. (*Ex 1130-53*)

Once part of the Dartmouth Estate, Farnley Tyas has retained much of its historic charm. Estate residents paid their rents in the Golden Cock. The farm on the left is one of the many dairy farms in the village. In a feature on the village in May 1947, Joe Brook (a 71-year-old farmer) said 'I don't think there's a village in Yorkshire with so little acreage and yet so many cattle'. (*Ex 3378-51*)

Seventy-five-year-old Mr W.Shaw of Church Terrace, Butts Road demonstrates the Farnley Tyas Parish Pump in May 1947 which had been disused for some time. (*Ex 1173-47*)

The former Thurstonland and Farnley Tyas Council met in this 'Old Council Room' in Thurstonland. Photographed in April 1954
villagers periodically still used the room to pay their rates and electricity bills. (*Ex 2217-54*)

Thurstonland was reported as the 'healthiest village in England' in January 1947 – but no new houses had been built for at least 50 years. The main street through the village in 1955. (*Ex 4815-55*)

'Sweeping Views and Quaint Corners' was the heading used in 1953 to describe Hepworth, a village of winding lanes. (*Ex 3069-53*)

Children playing in a quiet corner of Hepworth in 1953. (*Ex 3095-53*)

The road through Jackson Bridge in 1947. (*Ex 929-47*)

A country road near Jackson Bridge shows little had changed in 1958. (*Ex 4166-58*)

Four-year-old John Christopher Hamer of St George's Road is playing in one of the back alleys of Scholes in 1956. (*Ex 5091-56*)

The village of Paris near Scholes had its moment of fame when Mr Len Carter appeared on the television programme *What's My Line* in February 1954. Mr Carter defeated the panel with his job as a 'jerry operator' a process involved in the finishing of cloth. (*Ex 492-54*)

Honley, looking towards Trinity Church (now a United Reformed and Methodist Church) at the junction of Westgate with West Avenue and Moorbottom. (*Ex 4025-51*)

Mr Hirst Walker of Honley at the well in November 1951. A 90-year-old who said that he 'may retire in five years time'. He was still helping on his grandson's poultry farm after a lifetime spent in the textile industry. (*Ex 3893-51*)

'Mid the quietude of Honley's by-ways', Magdale. The old mill in the background was still inhabited on the lower floors but the upper storey was used as a store when this photograph was taken in 1952. (*Ex 3450-52*)

The centre of Holmfirth seen from Rotcher shows the junction of Dunford Road and Station Road in January 1957. (*Ex 426-57*)

Frank Taylor's 'quaint little cooked meat shop' was pictured near the town centre of Holmfirth only a few months after he had taken it over in 1956. (*Ex 422-57*)

Bank Lane, Holmbridge in 1952, the building on the right became the Fernleigh House restaurant. (*Ex 977-52*)

Haigh Howard, an 86-year-old shepherd, enjoying his *Examiner* at home in Holme village in January 1956. Ranges had been used for heating and cooking for over 100 years but by the 1950s they were being replaced by gas and electricity. Rag rugs were popular in the early years of the century in this part of the West Riding. (*Ex 259-56*)

Television came to the Huddersfield area in 1951 with the completion of the masts on Holme Moss. Pictured in May, a maintenance platform and secondary mast were all that was required before radio transmissions could begin in July and television in October 1951 serving 11 million people in the north of England. (*Ex 1628-51*)

Bottoms Mill dam seen from the road at Burnlee in May 1953. (*Ex 2109-53*)

Near Holmfirth the road winds through Burnlee towards Parkhead. Pictured in May 1953, the footbridge connects a house on one side of the road with its garden on the other. (*Ex 2108-53*)

'The country had been blanketed by snow – again but the landlord of the Isle of Skye reported it had stopped snowing and the road was open – a strong north-westerly was blowing and it was bitterly cold'. Six feet drifts in the hotel yard and seven degrees of frost overnight had added to the misery of February 1948. The Isle of Skye was closed and demolished in the 1950s because of pollution risks to the newly opened Digley Reservoir. (*Ex 2979A-48*)

'Hill road in the grip of winter'. The road to Upperthong in December 1950 as it climbs before its descent into Honley. (*Ex 14489-50*)

Wilshaw in the snow on the last day of 1950. (*Ex 14487-50*)

On 14 November 1953 the *Examiner* reported the 'Meltham Bus Stop Battle'. Traffic problems and risks to the public had caused an outcry against the position of the bus stop in the Market Place. (*Ex 4972-53*)

Ninety-year-old Miss Thermutas Dawson was Meltham's oldest resident on her birthday in November 1949. A cotton mill worker, she had been a lifelong teetotaller and a regular attender at her local Methodist Church. (*Ex 9525-49*)

'A hamlet enfolded in country quietude, this is Helme. No Post Office, even the two public houses are almost on the boundary'. Described by the *Examiner* in July 1952, Slades Lane and the village had changed little in recent years. (*Ex 3048-52*)

Canal and industry meet in the valley at Marsden. The canal bridges were designed to allow the horses pulling barges to pass underneath so that they did not need unharnessing. (*Ex 3146-52*)

Colne Valley Civic procession through the centre of Marsden in 1952. (*Ex 2340-52*)

Globe Farm on Manchester Road at Standedge in April 1952. The advertising hoardings were considered a safety hazard and by October 1953 the Standedge road was reported in the *Examiner* as 'the problem road of the north'. (*Ex 1522-52*)

Slaithwaite's 'Satanic Mills' taken from Manchester Road in August 1950. (*Ex 12972-50*)

Folly Dolly Falls, near Meltham Mills were so named after a 'Dolly' who made a bad property deal. (*Ex 1571-52*)

David Sheriff (of Moldgreen) travelled as a knife grinder and iron monger throughout the rural villages of this area. Seen here at work in Slaithwaite on 20 May 1953, he had served in Burma and as a result of his sufferings, unfortunately died a few months later. (*Ex 2153-53*)

Slaithwaite canal looking towards Carr Lane. In May 1953 the Examiner reported that a £14,000 scheme had been approved to drain and fill in the canal, demolish the bridge and widen Carr Lane and Old Bank. (*Ex 1953-53*)

Crimble looking towards Pole Moor in September 1951. (*Ex 3071-51*)

Christmas supplies being taken by horse and cart, driven by Jack Gledhill, to Cop Hill above Slaithwaite on 21 December 1950. At the time, the village had no electricity with many houses lit by candle or gas, water obtained from nearby streams, and no telephone or shops. (*Ex 14406-50*)

Kenneth Sedgewick walking up Chapel Hill in Linthwaite to read gas meters in July 1956. On his right is the Linthwaite County Junior School. (*Ex 3309-56*)

View of Colne Valley from Quarmby in August 1953. The lack of smoke from the mill chimneys suggests that this picture was taken during the Huddersfield Holiday Weeks. (*Ex 3731-53*)

Golcar from Share Hill in 1953. (*Ex 2114-53*)

According to legend, Golcar's New York district was named by an American doctor who settled in the area. (*Ex 1986-54*)

Ridings Lane is one of the 'labyrinth of cobbled streets winding up and down' the village of Golcar. The lane was frequently used by large lorries in 1957. (*Ex 1028-57*)

At 1,246 feet above sea level Scapegoat Hill was noted for its nonagenarians in 1947 when this picture of the New Inn was taken. (*Ex 980-47*)

'The well that never runs dry' was a lifesaver for the inhabitants of Scapegoat Hill during the drought of 1949. Mrs A.Shepherd is seen collecting water for use at home from the spring which flowed at 1,200 feet above sea level. (*Ex 8723-49*)

View from Scapegoat Hill across to Oakes and Salendine Nook in October 1956. (*Ex 4984-56*)

A popular place to visit on a day out, Pole Moor and Nont Sarah's were reported as being served by very few buses in 1955. These home comers are arriving on the late afternoon bus. (*Ex 4645-55*)

Mrs E.Holmes serves Mr A.Bard of Golcar in the cafe and general store at Pole Moor in October 1955. (*Ex 4643-55*)

Rural and Industrial Huddersfield

Taken in 1948 this photograph shows Fred Battye and his two horses as he took part in the National Farmers Union ploughing competition at Thurstonland. (*Ex 5061B-48*)

The Champion Tractor Ploughman award and Silver Challenge Cup were won by John Horsefield of Wolley near Barnsley at the NFU competition at Thurstonland in 1948. (*Ex 5060B-48*)

Fire workers helped to bring in the much needed harvest after the early bad weather of 1948. Wilf Armitage of Dogley Farm at Fenay Bridge is seen carrying a fork full of oats. (*Ex 4614-48*)

Mechanisation helped speed the harvest as corn was trussed beyond New Mill in August 1948. The *Examiner* reported that 'Gales the week previous had done a fair amount of damage even so returns above the average were forecast – if the heavens were kind'. (*Ex 4612-48*)

This Model 'T' Ford had been used since 1936 to carry the hay back to the barn at Lower House Farm. (*Ex 2597-51*)

Castle Hill from Benomley Woods with the oats 'stooked' to dry as straw in the early 1960s. (*GRS 700*)

Potato picking counted as lessons for these children from Skelmanthorpe Modern School in October 1948 as they worked for James Willey of Flockton Green. Left to right are Gladys Lind, Rex Booth, Bernard Ibbotson, Brian Schofield, Geoffrey Garside, Doreen Lambert and Mavis Feen. (*Ex 4998-48*)

For a number of years after the end of the Second World War, meat was rationed. In October 1953 it was reported that meat would be in short supply 'until after Christmas'. Christmas dinners were eagerly anticipated and each year flocks of turkeys graced the pages of the *Examiner*. These turkeys awaited their fate in fields near Meltham in November 1951. (*Ex 4110-51*)

These pigs are receiving 'tender loving care' from Mr Wilf Beaumont at Ashes Farm on Castle Hill in March 1956. In six weeks they would go to market. (Ex 1005-56)

J.A.Haigh feeding his sheep in the snows of February 1954. (*Ex 444-54*)

Harden Moss Sheepdog Trials still test the skills of farmers and shepherds every year. These sheep were being shorn in June 1956.
(*Ex 2822-56*)

Cows at Woodend Farm, Shepley. George T.Haigh had transformed the farm over the previous ten years. (*Ex 11078-50*)

'Their Milky Way', cows are led out near the Wappy Springs Inn on Lindley Moor Road through the snow in December 1951. (*Ex 4311-51*)

Milk was collected from the farms around Huddersfield by the Milk Marketing Board in milk churns such as these. John Robert Flint of Bank Top Farm, Marsden is leaving his churns at the side of the road by Hey Green Farm in October 1955. (*Ex 4766-55*)

The new 'attested' cattle market in Holmfirth was opened in September 1951 for the weekly sales. (*Ex 3383-51*)

Dives House Barn, photographed in 1949, contains good examples of the sixteenth-century 'Cruck' beams holding up the roof. (*Ex 8252-49*)

Mr Arthur Dawson, a Meltham blacksmith, was reported in the *Examiner* as only shoeing a few horses a year when this photograph was taken in June 1953. (*Ex 2879-53*)

Harold Armitage had run a one man lathe making workshop in Kirkheaton since 1935. This photograph was taken on 21 March 1956. (*Ex 1123-56*)

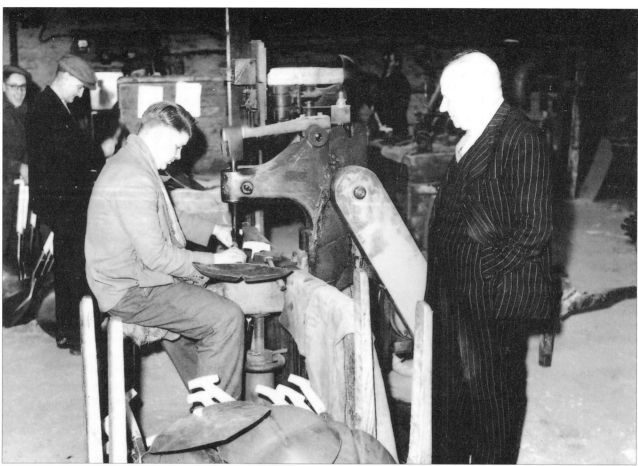

Stanley Carter (right) watches Ian Thompson at work in the 'department where shovels are completed' at Messrs Richard Carter Ltd. of Kirkburton. Founded in 1740 the third generation of the Carter family were still working in iron and other metals when this photograph was taken in April 1956. (*Ex 1807-56*)

Messrs George Lindley and Sons Ltd. had run the Sovereign Quarries at Shepley for 190 years in 1952. (*Ex 3101-52*)

Harold Morton moulding clay on the wheel in January 1956. His family had worked in the Lindley Moor Pottery for over 450 years. (*Ex 223-56*)

Edmund Taylor (Teasel) Ltd. of Moldgreen supplied teasels to all parts of the world when they celebrated 100 years in October 1949. Teasels are used in the woollen industry to raise a pile on high quality cloth. (*Ex 8980-49*)

Clough House Mill, Slaithwaite in 1949 was quoted by the *Examiner* as a perfect example of how the industrial revolution had affected the Colne Valley. (*Ex 7164-49*)

Brooke's Mills at Armitage Bridge in 1950. (*Ex 11817-50*)

The Titanic Mills of the Colne Valley Spinning Company near Linthwaite, were built at the same time as the Titanic, the 'unsinkable' ship which went down having struck an iceberg. (*Ex 1811-55*)

Machinery for carding wool at Lawton Spinning Mills on Firth Street in 1950. (*Ex 13852-50*)

Workers were photographed in August 1954 as they returned from their annual holidays to work in the pipecleaner manufacturing department at John L.Brierley's of Quay Street. (*Ex 4327-54*)

Miss Mary Sabina Pillings was still at the loom after 25 years working for Messrs Liddle and Brierley Ltd. Stanley Mills in Marsh. At 75 she still wore clogs and acted as 'knocker-up' for her neighbours. (*Ex 4978-48*)

John Taylor's Ltd. was described as 'a firm which has never lowered its standards' the girls in the mending room were 'still vital to high standards of production'. (*Ex 7851-49*)

'Lunch time at Milnsbridge'. Workers at the Union Mills of Messrs John Crowther & Sons (Milnsbridge) cross the bridge over the canal on their way to the canteen. (*Ex 1814-55*)

Henry Ramsden of Sellers setting shears during Huddersfield Holiday Weeks in August 1948. While the workers were away on holiday, the machinery received an annual overhaul. (*Ex 4396-48*)

Sellers at Folly Hall was described as having 'smoke blackened buildings (that) border the canal'. Since this photograph was taken in 1955 the works have expanded over the canal. (*Ex 1785-55*)

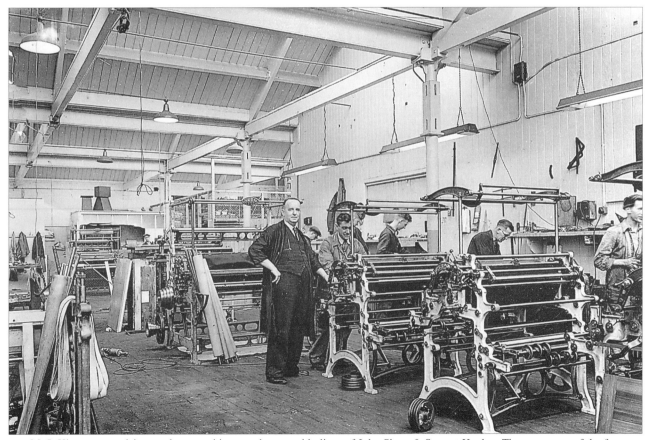

Mr L.Kippax supervising work on machines on the assembly lines of John Shaw & Sons at Honley. They were one of the few companies that printed the ruled pages in account and exercise books. (*Ex 8927-49*)

These electrical motors manufactured at the Empress Works of Brook Motors were destined for America. Mr N.Lindley (left) and Mr J.Cain are seen working on motors on the conveyer belt in November 1953. (*Ex 5203-53*)

Mr Douglas Evans, a hobbing machine operator at David Brown Gears Park Works, was looking forward to setting off for Switzerland at the start of the Engineering Holidays in July 1954. (*Ex 3612-54*)

David Brown's Tractor works in Meltham received many visitors in the drive for exports. This 1950 delegation included the ambassadors from Argentina and Venezuela. (*Ex 12579-50*)

L.B.Holliday's chemical works viewed from the bridge at Bradley in May 1953. (*Ex 2040-53*)

Mrs Dorothy Couchman packing dyestuff crystals for export to the bazaar trade of the Middle East and India. In September 1949 it was reported that she was one of the women who had continued to work at ICI since the war. (*Ex 8725-49*)

Emley Moor Colliery was just one of the many coal mines to the east of Huddersfield. They included Shuttle Eye, Grange Ash, Caphouse, Park Mill and Denby Grange. In 1988 Caphouse Colliery became the home of the Yorkshire Mining Museum. (*Ex 1466-53*)

The Leeds Road gasometer in January 1954. The little train is on its way to collect coal from the railway goods yard. In 1994 part of the track is still visible on Beaumont Street near the Yorkshire Rider Bus Depot. (*Ex 318-54*)

The Huddersfield Power Station viewed from Kilner Bank in 1953. Two of the new 250 foot high cooling towers had been completed but the old wooden ones were still in use. (*Ex 1173-53*)

Messrs D.Battey & Son Ltd. was founded in 1875 as a tallow candle maker but soon expanded to the manufacture of lubricating oils. The firm had offices in Henry Street and these storage tanks at Stoney Battery on Manchester Road. (*Ex 2215-53*)

Standard Fireworks at Crosland Moor exported 50 per cent of output in 1948, helping 'to pay for our food'. Vera Clayton is seen with the boxes ready to go out. A standard box of fireworks cost 2s. 6d. (13p). (*Ex 4936-48*)

Bentley & Shaw's Lockwood Brewery was founded in 1795 by Timothy Bentley. Pictured in January 1950, the brewery became offices and a distribution centre before it finally closed in November 1962. (*Ex 10060-50*)

Full bottles of orange crush are being loaded by Miss Lilian Hodgson and Mrs Doreen Robinson at Shaw's Mineral Waters based in Birkby on 26 November 1955. The company was founded in 1871 as brewers of 'botanic beer'. (*Ex 5306-55*)

Lawrence Batley coined the phrase 'cash and carry' when he opened his first warehouse in Sheepridge in 1958. The premises on Leeds Road were opened in 1962 and the firm is one of the most successful cash and carry wholesale distributors in the country. (*Ex 3836-62*)

Mr Arthur L.Woodhead was the Chairman of the Directors of Joseph Woodhead & Sons Ltd. in 1951. The *Huddersfield Examiner* was founded by his grandfather in 1851. (*Ex 3267-51*)

Miss Ethel Shinton retired after 41 years working for the GPO switchboard. Starting with just 12 telephonists in 1908 there were over 1,000 by 1949. The busiest day she remembered was Armistice Day in 1918. (*Ex 6034-49*)

The *Examiner* celebrated it's centenary in 1951 with the publication of a 'Special' which included a wide range of photographs. Methods of newspaper production have changed rapidly since this photograph of a Linotype machine operated by Walter S.Whiteley was taken. Lines of text were cast in hot metal and arranged into columns and pages for printing. (*Ex 3226-51*)

On 6 November 1953 the front page of the *Examiner* changed drastically. Before this date the first page of the newspaper contained only advertisements. Maurice Bentley (deputy overseer), George Chadwick (overseer – hand composition) and Bill Lowis (chief sub-editor) are pictured preparing the 'first' front page to contain news stories. (*Ex 4962-53*)

Examiner vans line up awaiting the first edition outside the Ramsden Street offices in June 1951. (*Ex 1973-51*)

Transport

Road Safety has always been an emotive issue and was emphasised in 'Accident Prevention Week' in August 1952. This sign on Leeds Road welcomed visitors to the town. (*Ex 3336-52*)

Pedestrians on zebra crossings caused rush hour traffic jams on New Street which was known as 'Nightmare alley' before the introduction of Police control in January 1952. (*Ex 205-52*)

Edwin Atkinson of Lowerhouses was invited to drive the State Coach of the Duke and Duchess of Devonshire in the Coronation procession in June 1953. (*Ex 1444-53*)

New coal hoppers erected at Aspley Basin in 1949 were expected to save time loading and unloading coal. (*Ex 9386-49*)

Keith France and two-year-old Dolly from Prospect Farm make their way along Moor Hill Road in Salendine Nook delivering the milk. In January 1956 the use of horse and cart was considered to be 'old fashioned'. (*Ex 224-56*)

Meanwhile Sam Waddington commenced his deliveries in the Sheepridge area with this 'new' electric float in April 1956. (*Ex 1594-56*)

This new *Examiner* van was photographed on 11 March 1947. (*Ex 686-47*)

White and Lockwood's garage on Bradford Road featured in the *Examiner's* 'Budget Special'. Petrol prices were raised by 7½d. to 4s. 3d. (21¼p) per gallon in the Budget of 13 March 1952. Mr Tom Grogan serves petrol watched by the car owner and Mr Norman Lockwood. (*Ex 917-52*)

'Two wheeled "old crock" has sprung to life again'. Colin Schofield of Wiley Brothers in Trinity Street was repairing a Fearnought cycle built in Huddersfield by Havilland & Armitage in 1905. The bicycle had been found in the underdrawing of Edgerton Post Office and was later donated to the Raleigh Museum in Nottingham. (*Ex 581-59*)

John Netherwood and mechanic Reggie Oakes were on their way to compete in the 350 cc class clubmans' Manx Grand Prix on the Isle of Man in August 1948. (*Ex 4591-48*)

Tramcar No. 27 on Lidget Street, Lindley in the early 1900s. Huddersfield Corporation opened the first municipal transport service in Britain in January 1883 with a steam tramcar travelling from Fartown to Lockwood. The Lindley route was opened in June 1883 and electrified in 1901. The trams were replaced by trolleybuses in November 1934. One of the few tram shelters (similar to the one on the left) to have survived can be found on Edgerton Road. (*SC.CO25.1962*)

Decorated by the Passenger Transport Department in celebration of the Coronation of Her Majesty Queen Elizabeth II, this trolley bus made its first appearance to the public on the 11.29am run to Crosland Moor on 30 May 1953. (*Ex 2353-53*)

Bus driver S.Bell using the mirror at Longroyd Bridge depot that helped to ensure the 'neatness and tidiness of all platform staff'. The mirror is now on display in the Transport Gallery at Tolson Museum. (*Ex 5081-53*)

Iris Parker was one of the 150 conductresses employed by Huddersfield Corporation Transport in 1953. (*Ex 5080-53*)

The staff at Huddersfield Corporation Transport joined a national bus strike in October 1949. Many people were forced to walk to work including these pictured on Chapel Hill. (*Ex 9040-49*)

Due to a shortage of staff, Brook Motors bought this bus in October 1948 to 'shuttle' girls between Huddersfield and their homes in Barnsley. (*Ex 5000-48*)

Ward's coaches based at the Red Lion Garage in Lepton served the area for many years. A passenger complained that it was 'too draughty inside the coach' and Dennis Ward is pictured checking the air vent on 7 December 1956. (*Ex 5427-56*)

Huddersfield Station had provided train booking and parcel facilities for local people for over 100 years. In 1954 there were 164 trains scheduled at the station in the winter timetable and 174 (going up to 211 on Saturdays) in the summer. Mass exoduses took place each year during Huddersfield Holiday Weeks.

Rail fares went up in September 1947.
A Third Class monthly return to Blackpool cost 19s. 1d.(95p); to Leeds 4s. 11d.(24p)

Robert Allen of Mirfield had been ticket collector at Huddersfield Station for over twenty years in August 1948. The station was poised for the mass exodus of Huddersfield Holiday Week. (*Ex 4325-48*)

Herbert Boothroyd and Arthur Mellor inside No I box at Huddersfield Station on 7 April 1954. (*Ex 1723-54*)

The water tower on platform 4 at Huddersfield Station was used to refill the boilers of steam trains. (*Ex 1736-54*)

The South Yorkshireman rushes across Lockwood viaduct in December 1956. (*Ex 5469-56*)

'Farewell old faithfuls' – Bess, Dolly and Tommy were made redundant from Huddersfield Station in November 1952. Bred in the Huddersfield area these horses had to be at least 15 cwt. before the railway would buy them. The men who looked after them were Richard Gibson, Thomas Shaughnessy and John Fowler. (*Ex 5060-52*)

A British Railway goods delivery van in Lowerhouses. Walter Tansey of Outlane drove one of these vans which replaced the heavy horses. (*Ex 5298-56*)

Fires and Disasters

On 13 May 1948 the *Examiner* reported that 'the driver and fireman of a coal train leapt from the footplate seconds before their engine collided with the rear of empty passenger coaches at Heaton Lodge Junction'. (*Ex 3588-48*)

A Dakota aeroplane crashed on the hills above the Isle of Skye in 1949 resulting in the death of 23 people. Survivors were stretchered out by mountain rescue teams and taken to Oldham Royal Infirmary. (*Ex 8355-49*)

Fire followed an explosion in the purifying plant at Huddersfield Gasworks on 23 July 1948. The town's gas supply was not disrupted although staff expected to suffer because their work would be made more difficult by the damage it had caused. (*Ex 4188-48*)

Upper Aspley Mills were destroyed by fire in June 1954. Over 60 firemen from around the area fought the blaze at the premises of Messrs John Eccles Ltd. (*Ex 2801-54*)

Fire swept through the furniture department on the top floor of Beaumont's warehouse in Victoria Lane resulting in £30,000 damage. The lower floors were reopened within a few days. According to the *Examiner* report on 20 May 1954 other premises affected by water included Fairburn's leather shop. (*Ex 2603-54*)

Four houses were destroyed in L.B.Holliday's tip fire at Deighton in September 1955. The fire was reported to have been 'like a volcano eruption'. (*Ex 4433-55*)

Fires raging on the moors around Huddersfield as a result of the drought in July 1949 encircling the cafe and house at Buckstones. (*Ex 7715-49*)

Flood damage at the entrance of Standedge Tunnel. The National Fire Service pumped out water near Tunnel End. The Colne and Holme Valleys were also affected by the sudden downpours of 20 September 1946. (*Ex 8-46*)

The roof of several mills collapsed under the weight of snow in March 1947 including Crimble Mill at Slaithwaite. The *Examiner* also reported that many villages were still isolated, phones out of order and food rations in danger. (*Ex 696-47*)

Flood chaos lasted for several days during the thaw following the heavy snows of 1947. The mill yard of Crowther Bruce & Co. in Marsden needed sweeping out on 17 March. Gas had been cut off by the floods and the country as a whole was still suffering regular electricity power cuts. (*Ex 708-47*)

Medical and Social Services

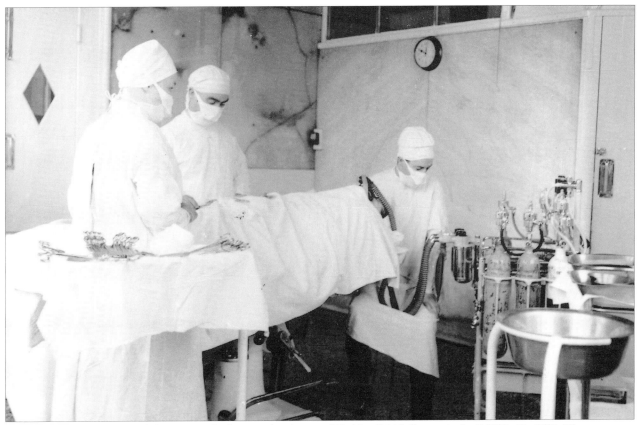

Sister Sharrett and the surgeons in the operating theatre of Huddersfield Infirmary in April 1953. (*Ex 1001-53*)

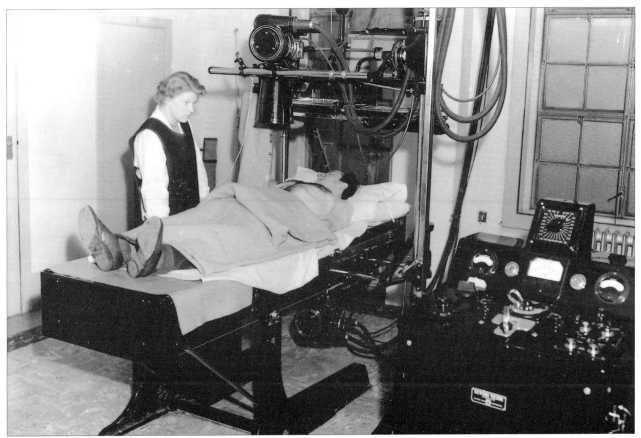

The X-ray Department in the Huddersfield Infirmary was reported as having treated 18,266 patients in 1952. The radiologist Miss J.M.Thackery is pictured X-raying Mr Stanislaus Nowak in April 1953. (*Ex 1077-53*)

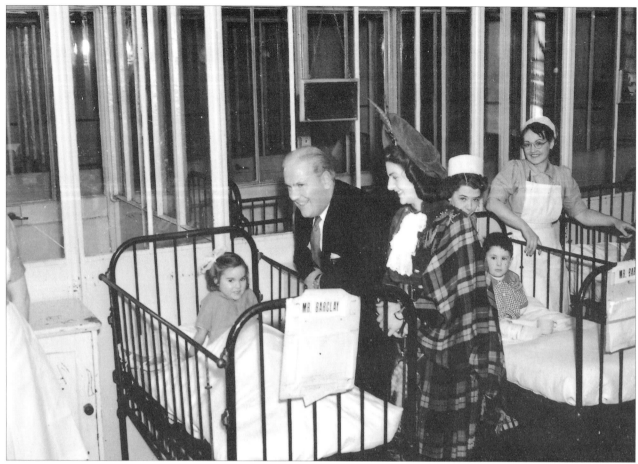

Carrol Lewis and singer Rosemary MacKay at the bedside of Dianne Bedford of New Mill during their visit to the children's ward at the Royal Infirmary in December 1950. (*Ex 14313-50*)

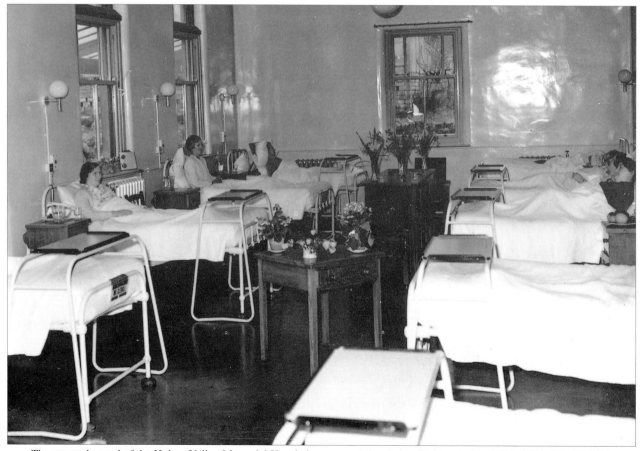

The women's ward of the Holme Valley Memorial Hospital was reported as being 'light and cheerful' in 1954. (*Ex 1389-54*)

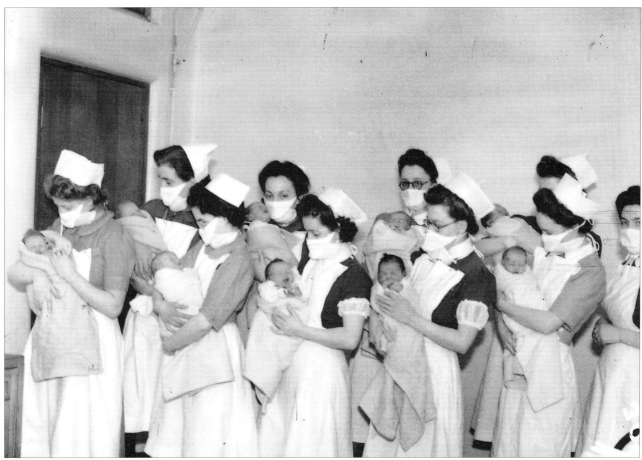

Leap Year babies born on 29 February 1948 at the Princess Royal Maternity Home included babies Robinson, Herbert, Briggs, Arnott, Secker, Hopkinson, Sharp, Dews, and Holroyd. Mrs Moss of Newsome bore twins at St Lukes Hospital on the same day. (*Ex 3023-48*)

A New electro-Encephalograph costing £1,500 was installed at Storths Hall Hospital in 1949. It was intended to help cure 'brain illness'. (*Ex 5992-49*)

Sister C.Smith supervises 110 patients in Ward 6 at Storths Hall Hospital. Television was available on all wards by January 1954. (*Ex 176-54*)

Stirring the gravy at Storths Hall Hospital are Mrs A.Foster, Miss K.Lord and Mrs E.Mellor in January 1954. (*Ex 163-54*)

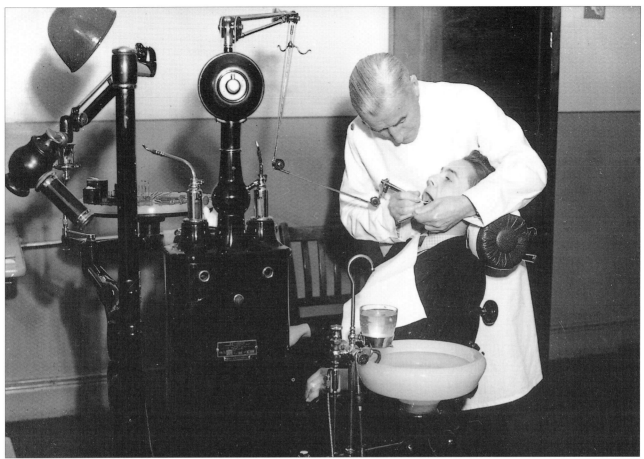

Mr A.B.Sheilds is working on 14-year-old David Rothwell at the Huddersfield Clinic. The Dentistry Department was reported as 'sadly understaffed' in October 1953. (*Ex 4683-53*)

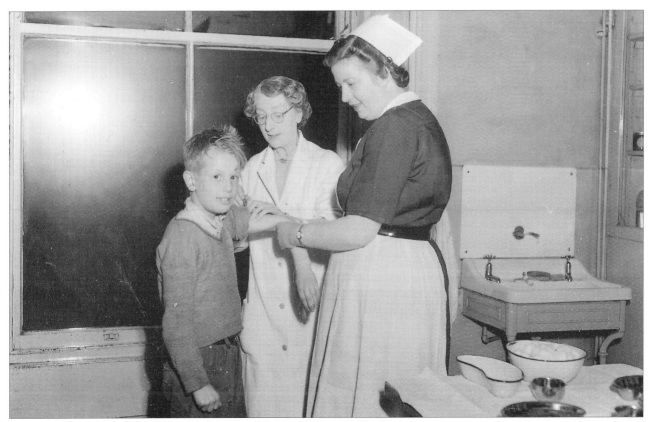

Poliomyelitis epidemics had taken 18 lives in the Huddersfield area in 1949, ten cases were reported in 1955. Parents queued for hours to register their children for the newly developed vaccine in March 1956. The first delivery of vaccine arrived in May and Dr Dorothy Thompson and Nurse Mrs C.Mary Sutton (née Wilson) are seen vaccinating Stewart Norman Ferguson, the first of many children against poliomyelitis. (*Ex 2003-56*)

An outbreak of smallpox in Britain in January 1962 caused panic. Many Huddersfield people queued for hours outside the Council Offices in Ramsden Street for their chance to be vaccinated against this serious disease which by the 1990s had been eliminated throughout the world. (*Ex 181-62*)

The Meals on Wheels service was introduced on 28 September 1949. Early customers queued in Kirkgate to collect the first meals, which cost one shilling (5p), to take to invalids. Mrs C.Farington, Mrs J.Knockton, Mrs A.Dunne are served by Mrs A.Highley. (*Ex 8977-49*)

In May 1953 the WRVS opened a new headquarters on Church Street. The photograph shows (left) Mrs F.A.Hall, Mrs J.Longbotton and Mrs T.F.Cliffe (rear) in the clothing store which has helped many needy families over the years. (*Ex 1999-53*)

A new Workshop for the Blind was opened on 13 November 1952. Mr H.Pickering is weaving a flower basket. Included in the *Examiner*, on the day this photograph was published, was a 'Plea to parents' asking them not to allow children to use the railings leading to the entrance for 'acrobatic games'. (*Ex 4834-52*)

Education and Youth Work

Southgate Nursery celebrated Christmas with a tea party and entertainment in December 1948. (*Ex 5455-48*)

'Are children getting enough to eat?' was the question asked on a number of occasions in 1948 as rations were reduced yet again. These children at Spring Grove School seem to have a plateful and 'get second helpings too'. (*Ex 5260-48*)

'Representing a new era', studies in concentration during morning milk break as children consume their third of a pint of milk in 1954. Opened in 1951, Dalton Junior School was the first of the new schools to be built in Huddersfield. (*Ex 880-54*)

Miss Gent and Miss H.M.Castle supervise activities at this physical education lesson at Moldgreen Infants School. (*Ex 662-54*)

Pupils at Woodhouse School designed and built a model bungalow as part of their work during their 'extra' year at school in 1948. Changes to the school leaving age meant that children could not leave school at 14 but had to wait until they were 15 years old. (*Ex 4240-48*)

An *Examiner* series about education in 1954 featured several schools including Hillhouse Technical School. Headmaster Mr J.H.Housby (left) and Mr W.Waterhouse are pictured in the science laboratory during a fourth form chemistry lesson. (*Ex 553-54*)

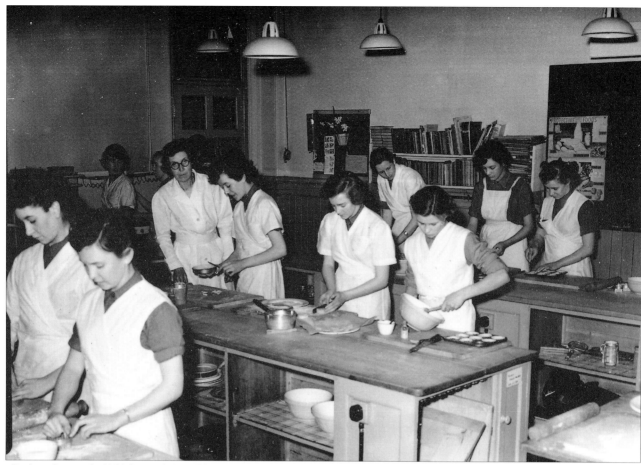

Cookery lessons in 1954 featured these fifth form girls at Greenhead High School as they prepare pastries under the direction of Miss Z.E.Hull. (*Ex 599-54*)

Huddersfield Town Hall was the regular venue for the annual Speech Day for many children attending Huddersfield secondary and grammar schools. These girls from Greenhead High School were presented with awards by Dr McKenzie in December 1948. (*Ex 5451-48*)

Rawthorpe Secondary School nearing completion in June 1952 was the first of the many 'new' secondary schools to be built in the post war years. (*Ex 2311-52*)

A number of new secondary schools were opened in the late 1950s and 1960s. Huddersfield Borough Corporation was proud to receive Princess Margaret to open the Salendine Nook Schools site in November 1958. (*Ex 4519-58*)

Huddersfield Technical College was opened in 1883 by the Duke of Somerset. From its origins as a Mechanics Institute in 1841 the Technical College became a Polytechnic and in 1993, a University. (*KCS*)

Huddersfield Technical College School of Art expanded into Milton Church School in 1948. There were 80 full time and 800 part-time students in the School of Art in November 1948. (*Ex 5325-48*)

The ladies woodworking class at Holmfirth Technical Institute in May 1953 was taught by Mr Griffiths. The class met on Tuesday evenings making mainly tea trolleys and trays. In the right foreground are Miss M.Hirst and Mrs L.Robinson. (*Ex 2030-53*)

At Birkby Youth Club's open night in May 1950 work undertaken through the year was exhibited. The main aims of the youth club were 'to teach the members to have a sense of responsibility, to hold new ideas and live amicably with others of their own age ... (and) at 21 have a sense of civic responsibility'. Left to right are Connie Hogan, Anne Beverley, Brenda Brooks, and Pauline Gover. (*Ex 11554-50*)

The Scouts at Milnsbridge Baptist Church celebrated their 30th anniversary in 1949. Harold Wilson enjoyed his time as a scout in Huddersfield with this troop. (*Ex 9462-49*)

Rodney Allen and Trevor Chappell of 43rd Huddersfield Scouts based at Crosland Moor delivered whitewash as part of their activities during 'Bob a Job' week in April 1953. (*Ex 1401-53*)

Huddersfield East District Rangers erect a tent at their Longley Hall Camp under the leadership of their captain Mrs Elsie Hughes and lieutenant Barbara Harris in 1949. (*Ex 7896A-49*)

'These young blue jackets practice under the eye of their instructor C.P.O. Paxman (seated). All the officers of "T.S. Nelson" have R. N. experience and the veteran sea dog of them all is Lt. W.Hoggarth who fought at Jutland in 1916. Lt. Burnett served on one of the destroyers in the Battle of the Atlantic in the World War Two.' The Sea Cadets met in their headquarters on what is now Old Leeds Road. C.P.O. Rutherford is standing while the boys learn their Morse code. (*Ex 1257-53*)

Cultural Life

Huddersfield Library was opened in 1940. In many ways the building has not altered but the service has adapted to the increased expectations of the public.

The Childrens' library was very popular in 1953. Four staff regularly issued over 1000 books on a Saturday (children were only allowed one story book and two true books each at a time). The murals by C. P. Napier represented various 'local' legends, such as the Marsden Cuckoo and the Slaithwaite Moonrakers. (*Ex 4776-53*)

Huddersfield Reference Library in October 1953 was reported as having over 12,000 reference books. (*Ex 4865-53*)

The Huddersfield Art Gallery which was founded in 1898 moved to the top floor of the Huddersfield Library building in 1943. The Art Gallery's 'prize' possession in 1953 was this head of 'Einstein' by Epstein, purchased by the town in 1951. (*Ex 4864-53*)

Sir Malcolm Sargent's 'unparalleled service to music' resulted in him becoming a Freeman of the Borough of Huddersfield on 13 October 1961. Sir Malcolm Sargent is on the left with the Mayor Ald. H.F.Brook and Mr G.D.A.Heywood, President of the Huddersfield Choral Society. (*Ex 3476-61*)

Huddersfield Choral Society and Sir Malcolm Sargent take a bow at a performance of the *Messiah* in December 1961. (*Ex 3477-61*)

Mr W.G.Williams, the Music Advisor to Huddersfield Education Authority brought together children at Springwood School to form the first of the Huddersfield Youth Orchestras in July 1950. (*Ex 12152-50*)

Brass bands have been popular in this area for many years. The Skelmanthorpe Band dates from 1820s and was reported in a weekly series on brass bands in 1956 as having a very good record of successes in 'the Post-War'. Back row: (left to right) M.Shaw, B.Lodge, B.Inglesfield, D.Hey, G.Tricket, J.Copley, T.Stephenson, G.Whittles, R.Eastwood, R.Fisher, L.Mann, R.Allott, S.Gill. Front row: H.Eastwood, G.Bond, G.Taylor, R.Radley, T.E.Field (President), H.Millerman (Conductor), F.Wood, E.Wood, J.Hirst, B.Haigh, H.Ramsden, C.Hawkins. (*Ex 5064-56*)

'Music while you work' – not the radio programme but a talent contest arranged by the workers in David Brown's canteen at Park Works on 22 November 1948. (*Ex 5286-48*)

The Theatre Royal on Ramsden Street was the home of Huddersfield's professional theatre but it was also used by many of the local amateur groups. The Huddersfield Thespians presented Noel Coward's *Present Company* in December 1959. The photograph shows (from the left) Mary Crossley, Philip Hillaby and Doreen Shaw. (*Ex 3870-59*)

Roy Castle, born in Scholes above Holmfirth, was at the top of a variety bill at the Ritz before setting off to the London Palladium in February 1959. (*Ex 624-59*)

James Mason born in Marsh in 1909 was the star of many Hollywood films including *The Seventh Veil* and was nominated for an Oscar for best supporting actor in *The Verdict*. He visited his mother in the spring of 1959. (*Ex 1093-59*)

'All roads led to the Ritz Cinema' in December 1953. The Cinderella Society invited 1000 children to its annual party where they watched cartoons and Laurel and Hardy films before receiving a small present to take home. (*Ex 5565-53*)

The circus was a regular visitor to town. Bertram Mills Circus horses rise to the occasion as an attraction 'greatly enjoyed by all' in July 1949. (*Ex 7794-49*)

Billy Smart's Circus parading for the last time to Greenhead Park having arrived at the station. This photograph was taken from an upstairs window at Wiley Brothers in Trinity Street. (*GRS 435*)

In June 1953, Billy Smart's circus advertised its 'Coronation Programme' in the *Huddersfield Daily Examiner*. The cost was 2s. to 10s. 6d. (10p to 52p) for the 1,000 unreserved seats; reserved seats cost between 4s. and 10s. 6d. (20p to 52p). The Sunday attraction was to be their arrival at the railway station 3pm on Sunday 14 June to parade up to Greenhead Park.

Holme Moss television went on the air at 10am on 15 August 1951. The first mention in the *Huddersfield Daily Examiner* of television programmes was on 12 October 1952. Commencing at 5.45pm 'For Children' closing at 10.15pm with weather, news and a sound only political broadcast. 'Entranced' children watching television are (seated) Helen Goldthorpe, Gay Dobson, (standing) John Goldthorpe and Elizabeth Haigh. (*Ex 2864-51*)

The Railway Circle's first exhibition was staged in April 1953 when they unveiled the 'Bruddersford Station on the West Yorkshire Railway'. W.Houghton and F.Sutcliffe show the layout to the Mayor, Ald. J.F.C.Cole. (*Ex 1354-530*)

Sports and Pastimes

Knur and Spell is an old Yorkshire game that was still played in Kirkheaton in April 1955 (*Ex 1586-55*)

A popular pastime for young and old, the Thornton Lodge v Crosland Moor over 65's Bowls took place on 28 July 1948. The oldest players on this day were J.Goddard (82) and A.Bates (78). (*Ex 4238-48*)

The Huddersfield and District Clay Pigeon Shooting Association, one of the few associations to keep going throughout the war, held regular meets at Fenay Bridge in the 1950s. (*Ex 11675-50*)

Spectators at the men's tennis final watch as J. Milton (of Mirfield) defeated H. Yates (a football player for Huddersfield Town) in the annual competition held in Greenhead Park as part of the 'Holidays at Home' season. (*Ex 4448-48*)

Huddersfield Cricket Festival in 1949 included the 'best match of the week' when the ladies of Yorkshire met the Combined Counties team. The second largest crowd of the week, 504 people paid a total of £23 for the privilege of watching a woman hit the quickest 50 runs of the festival. (*Ex 7921-49*)

The Lascelles Hall Cricket Club is one of the oldest in the area. The team pictured in June 1953 included Fred Whittle and Norman Castles. (*Ex 2801-53*)

Huddersfield Town Association Football Club commenced training in hot humid conditions with their new coach Alf Young and trainer Jack Martin (right) in July 1948. Left to right: Nightingale, Whittingham, Metcalfe, Percival, Battye, Senior, Boot and Bateman. (*Ex 4229-48*)

Denis Law signed 'on the dotted line' on Monday 25 February 1957. At 17 he became the youngest professional player in the Football League although he had made his debut for Huddersfield Town on 24 December 1956. The photograph shows Bill Shankly (standing), Denis Law, Mr H.Beever (secretary) and Mr A.Galvin (assistant secretary). (*Ex 899-57*)

Fartown won the Rugby League Championship on 14 May 1949 scoring 13-12 against Warrington. The picture shows on the left Bob Nicholson, Pat Devery with the ball and Lionel Cooper rushing to his rescue in the foreground. (*Ex 6544-49*)

Anne Hall, and her sister-in-law Mrs I.Hopkinson won the Ladies Cup in an RAC event in 1951. She went on to successfully compete in many rallys including the Monte Carlo. Photographed with her children following a visit to Monte Carlo in 1951. (*Ex 357-51*)

At 21 years old Anita Longsborough worked for Huddersfield Corporation but won gold medals for her country at the Olympic Games. She was featured in the *Examiner* in August 1962 having won a gold medal at the European Swimming Championships in Leipzig. (*Ex 3511-62*)

Derek Ibbotson ran through Delph Woods as part of his training in February 1959. Born at Berry Brow he was a member of the Longwood Harriers Athletic Club and broke the world record in 1957 when he ran a mile in 3 min 57.2 seconds. (*Ex 396-59*)

The *Daily Express* Cycle Race over Holme Moss in September 1953. (*Ex 4008-53*)

Cycle Cross was one of the few sports to survive the bad weather in February 1955. Brian Haskell is in the lead on the course at Sude Hill, unfortunately he had to withdraw later. (*GRS 572*)

Weather

In the 1940s and 1950s deep snow created many problems in winter and on a number of occasions was followed by drought in the summer.

Butcher's boy, Geoffrey Kaye, was delivering meat by sledge in Emley in February 1947 when the *Examiner* reporter arrived on the first bus into the village. It had been cut off by severe snow drifts which were dug out by hand and the village had been without power for several days. (*Ex 552-47*)

Snow drifts in Ashes Lane, Almondbury being cleared in 1954. The bus to Farnley Tyas became stuck in drifts in this area on a number of occasions in the 1940s and 50s. (*GRS 309*)

Ice surrounded the metalwork at the bottom of a cooling tower at the Huddersfield electricity power station in January 1954. (*Ex 416-54*)

The severe winters were on several occasions followed by very dry summers. The shortage of water during the 1949 drought resulted in Mr David Tweedy of Berry Lot Farm at Scammonden taking water to his livestock in a milk churn. (*Ex 7717-49*)

Serious fogs and smogs blanketed the country in November 1948. Although the Nag's Head at Lindley Moor on page 49, was in sunshine this trolleybus was led by a cyclist through the dense fog. (*Ex 5323-48*)

'This standpipe is one of 28 erected by the corporation to warn people of the consequences of not saving water'. Although it had rained the previous night Huddersfield had suffered three periods of absolute drought between 14 August and 11 October 1959. (*Ex 3244-59*)

Politics

The Young Conservatives supported J. Woods Smith, a candidate for the Huddersfield East constituency in June 1950 when they took this mobile cinema to the site of Huddersfield Open Market. Left to right are J.Woods Smith, Mrs Felicity Dawson, Miss Elizabeth Brierley, Mrs M.Gledhill and Mrs Mary Hirst. (*Ex 12013-50*)

Mrs Sarah Braithwaite with Richard Wainright, the Liberal candidate for the Holme Valley, during the 1959 parliamentary election campaign. (*Ex 2981-59*)

The Labour Party Gift day on 7 November 1959 was addressed by Huddersfield-born Harold Wilson, the then Labour Shadow Chancellor. He is seen here with and J.P.W.Mallalieu and David Sykes. (*Ex 3577-59*)

Special Events

The many War Memorials dedicated after the Second World War included this one at Thurstonland. The service was conducted by the Vicar, the Revd N.G.Hounsfield, whose son's name is included on the memorial. The address was given by Canon F.Woods of Huddersfield and the memorial unveiled by Lt. Col. S.R.Hoyle of the 7th Battalion Duke of Wellington Regiment on 9 September 1948. (*Ex 4802-48*)

A Territorial Army exhibition in October 1948 resulted in searchlights over the town for the first time since the war. This Comet tank rumbling through the streets could reach speeds of up to 30 miles per hour. (*Ex 5098-48*)

The exhibition also included V2 rockets which were displayed outside the Drill Hall. (*Ex 5101-48*)

Remembrance Day services were very important in the early years after the War. Representatives of many organisations, including the Huddersfield Fire Brigade and the Girl Guides, arrived at the Parish Church on 7 November 1948. (*Ex 5191-48*)

Huddersfield Borough confirmed the privilege on the Duke of Wellington Regiment of marching through the town with bayonets fixed, colours flying and bands playing on 13 September 1952. The regiment still recruits from the Huddersfield area. (*Ex 3976-52*)

The wedding of Princess Elizabeth to Prince Philip in 1948 was celebrated throughout the country. The wedding dress was displayed in many towns and cities raising money for charity. On the first day 3,859 visitors saw the display at the Huddersfield Electricity Showrooms in Market Street, raising £65 4s. 3d. (£65.21¼) for *Save the Children*. (*Ex 5203-48*)

Princess Elizabeth and Prince Philip visited Huddersfield on 26 July 1949. The crowds waited to welcome them on High Street. (*Ex 8011-49*)

The Royal party with Mr E.Overton at Learoyd Bros., Trafalgar Mills on Leeds Road. (*Ex 7975-49*)

The death of King George VI was marked in Huddersfield by large crowds standing in silence at 2 pm on 15 February 1952. The mayor and civic dignitaries joined 3,000 people attending the three memorial services, held simultaneously, in St Peter's Parish Church, St Paul's and the Queen Street Mission. (*Ex 504-52*)

Coronation Street Party, Central Avenue, Fartown. The children were allowed to keep the Coronation mugs as souvenirs after their party on Saturday 6 June 1953. (*Ex 2591-53*)

Throughout the country towns and villages decorated the streets to celebrate the Coronation of Queen Elizabeth II. In the Huddersfield area they also held street parties, fancy dress parades and special bonfires although the weather was very wet. The children of the Netherthong village school celebrated the Coronation with a fancy dress parade in 1953. (*Ex 2452-53*)

The Yearly Round

The Mayor's Ball was a glittering occasion when Cllr. & Mrs G.B.Jones welcomed the mayors of nine other towns and 700 guests on 18 January 1952. (*Ex 203-52*)

Revd R.R.Parry and members of Highfield Congregational Church celebrate Good Friday at their open air service at 3 p.m. on Castle Hill. The tradition of a Good Friday walk and service has continued since this, the first occasion in April 1947. Church members on the photograph include Miss Archer, Christine Dicks, Barbara Hallett, Ann Hardy, Bernard Kershaw, Barbara McKinna, Elsie Parry, John Parry, David Ritchie and Pat Schofield. (*Ex 801-47)*

A Good Friday service was held in the Market Place in April 1949. Similar services in the 1990s take place at the foot of a large cross on the Piazza. (*Ex 6667-49*)

Whitsuntide walkers wending their way from Slaithwaite Central Methodist Church down Manchester Road to their tea and field day on 30 May 1955. (*Ex 2359-55*)

Deighton Working Men's Club's procession passes along Deighton Road as part of the route of their annual 'walk' in 1949. The club ran a Waffin-Fuffen band for about five years in the 1940s and 1950s. (*Ex 7410-49*)

Huddersfield 'Holidays at Home' began in 1941 to entertain those who could not get away because of the war. Since then the season has gone from strength to strength. Entertainments ranged from simple games of draughts in Greenhead park to talent contests and shows. (*Ex 4443-48*)

Weather had been poor during the Huddersfield Holiday Weeks but the playground in Greenhead park was still very popular with the children in July 1951. (*Ex 2589-51*)

Hope Bank at Honley, opened in 1893 by William Mellor, included a fleet of 30 rowing boats and a pleasure steamer *Nil Desperandum*. They were complemented by pleasure gardens, dancing, swings and an amusement park which included the Hotchkiss Bicycle Railway and the Switchback. (*Ex 1235-47*)

In 1947 Hope Bank was taken over by Fred Thompson of Cleveley who installed speed boats, a helta skelta and a small zoo. Record crowds of 50,000 visited Hope Bank on Whit Monday 17 May 1948. In January 1951 Tasha the bear escaped from her cage. Although attempts were made by the RSPCA to persuade her to return they had to shoot her as darkness approached. The Gardens were no longer a going concern by 1955 and the area was bought by Brook Motors who drained the lake to build a factory. (*Ex 304-51*)

The annual Children's pet show run by the RSPCA attracted large crowds to St Paul's Drill Hall in September 1948. Mr J.W.North is pictured judging the best conditioned dog with short hair. (*Ex 4729-48*)

Above: The Chrysanthemum Show was held annually in the Huddersfield Town Hall where extravagant displays of colour were recorded each year. The display on the stage was prepared by the Corporation Parks Department under the direction of F.W.Martin (deputy Parks Superintendent). These blooms were grown at Ravensknowle Park by Mr T.F.Armitage (head gardener). Photographed in 1948, the Chrysanthemum Society celebrated its centenary in 1953. (*Ex 4712-48*)

Left: The gathering together of singers to raise money for charity is a local tradition which started in the township of Longwood. Known as 'the Mother of all Sings', Longwood Sing had been held on eighty-six occasions in the grounds of Nab End Tower by 1959. A total of £59 was collected, an increase of £20 on the previous year, by the singers whose repertoire included choruses from the *Messiah*. (*Ex 2749-59*)

Above: Stirring the Christmas pudding was a serious job for these children at Fieldhead Children's home in December 1950. (*Ex 14241-50*)

Left: Patricia Ann Sykes of Blackhouse Road, Fartown helps prepare the bonfire in November, 1948. The *Examiner* reported that shops were sold out of fireworks and that there were more guys in evidence. (*Ex 5173-48*)

'Diana Margaret Smith of Beaumont Park looks overwhelmed amongst so many toys, but seems to like the rocking horse', in the toy department of Rushworth's Department Store in November 1948. (*Ex 5301-48*)

Sorting the post at Huddersfield Post Office on 20 December 1948. On the peak day at the Huddersfield Post Office, 12,500 letters an hour were sorted. The main Post Office was open on Christmas Day for telegrams between 9.30 and 10.30 am and although a delivery was promised – there would be no collections. (*Ex 5448-48*)

The Christmas rush as shoppers hurry to buy last-minute bargains in the Shambles on 24 December 1952. (*Ex 5400-52*)

Father Christmas arrives by sledge to visit children at Kirkheaton Church School in December 1952. (*Ex 5268-52*)

'All set for Santa', Margaret and Peter Lockwood of Golcar were not worried about the problem caused to Santa by the modern fireplace. (*Ex 9849-49*)

Snow covers the Christmas tree in Huddersfield Market Place in December 1955. The lights had been switched on by the Mayor, Cllr. J.T.Gee. (*Ex 2615-55*)

Bibliography

Huddersfield Daily Examiner
Huddersfield Weekly Examiner
Beach, David T. ed. *Huddersfield Trolleybus Memories* (Huddersfield, 1983)
Brook. Roy *Huddersfield Corporation Tramways* (Huddersfield, 1983)
Haigh, E.A.H. *Huddersfield: A Most Handsome Town* (Huddersfield, 1992)
Hinchcliffe, Brian *Huddersfield in the Tramway Era* (Sheffield, 1978)
Historic Almondbury : The Village on the Hill (Huddersfield, 1975)
Holmes, D.H. *The Mining and Quarrying Industries in the Huddersfield District* (Huddersfield, 1967)
Shackleton, E. *A Living Inheritance* (Huddersfield, 1988)
Varley, W.J *Castle Hill* (Huddersfield, 1973)
Wyles, David *The Buildings of Huddersfield* (Huddersfield, 1985)

Copies of the above books may be consulted, borrowed or in some cases purchased from Huddersfield Library.

Subscribers

Sylvia Abele
Joyce Abbott
Alan Addy
Philip Addy
Alice Mary Ainley
C P Ainley
Margaret Ainley
Audrey & John Allen
Paul & Ceri Allen
Richard Allen
Bob Allsop
Bradley Archer
David Ulrich Armitage
Eileen Armitage
Frank Byron Armitage
George Armitage
Ian Armitage
Mr John D Armitage
Lilian Anitage
Lynda Armitage-Jones
M G & C M Armitage
Peter Armitage
Steven Armitage
A & J Armstrong
Sue Asher
Ronald Atkins
Mrs Shirley Atkins
Edward Avotins
G Ayers
Mr M Zubair Aziz
Peter J W Bailey
Norma Baimbridge
Geoffrey Baldwin
Robert Baldwin
Mr D H Ball
Colin Balmforth
Edward Bamforth
M Hemingway & A Bamforth
J D Bamforth
John Garside Bamforth
Peter G Barker
Revd. D Barraclough
Mrs Shirley Barraclough
Mr William Moorhouse Barrowclough
Roy C Bartholomew
Mr R A Battye
Rita & Ronald Battye
Barry Baxter
Herbert G Baxter
Brian Beaumont
Malcolm & Margaret Beaumont
Roy & Jill Beaumont
Susan Beaumont
Mr & Mrs W Beck
Peter H Beckett
Godfrey Bedford
Mr Dennis Bell
I G Bell
E Bellamy
Sheila Bellamy
H Bennett
Mr & Mrs M J Bennett
Mr Roy Bentley
George F Berry
Noel W Berry
Norman F Berry
Mr Roy Berry
Stanley Beveridge
Pawel Bialkowski
Susan Elizabeth Billington
J B Biltcliffe
K W Bilton
Mrs Mavis Binns
Joyce Birkett
Phillip John Birmingham
M J Black
Terry & Shirley Blackburn
Mr & Mrs H Blakeley
Revd. & Mrs J G Blakeley
Clive & Christine Blakey
Ian D Blakey
P Stuart Blakey
Derrick M Boardman

Joyce Bolton (*née* Rogers)
Alan Booth
Brian Booth
Mrs B Booth
Mr George Booth
Graham Spencer Booth
Martin A Booth
Mr R A Booth
William Booth
Mr Sydney Boothroyd
Mrs N Bostock
Mr Keith Bottom
J G Bottomley
Mr P Bottomley
Mrs Barbara Bower
Edith Bradbury
D M Bradley
Howard Bradley
Mrs Joan Bradley
Ron Bradley
John H Bramley
Mrs N Bray
Mr Terance Brennan
Mr & Mrs J Brier
J C Brierley
Peter Brierley
Raymond Brierley
George L Briggs
Harold Broadbent
Bernard & Ann Brook
Mr Eric Brook
Mr Harry Brook
Edward Brook & Honoria Brook
Maegan Jo Brook
Gordon R Brooke
Marcus W Brooke
Tim N K Brooke
W R Brothers
Miss Christine E Brown
Ethel D Brown
Mr & Mrs H S Brown
Mr Jack Brown
Mr J Roger Brown
Mr & Mrs L A Bruce
Alice Bull
John Bullock
Phyllis Burford
Jack Burgess
Shelley J Burgin
Trevor Burgin OBE
Mrs M Burhouse
D R Burke
G K N Burton
Mrs Jane Burton
James Bustard
Paul Butcher
Mr & Mrs Vincent & Doris Evelyn Butler
Patricia Butterfield
Sylvia Butterworth
Professor John Calam
Stephen Calverley
Gorrdon Carney
Mr & Mrs P J Carter
Robert A Carter
David B Cartwright
Mr & Mrs J Castle
J D Challand
Barry S Chambers
Mr Peter Chambers
P H Child
Roy Chilvers
William Clark
Mr & Mrs G S Clarke
John George Clarke
S A Clarke
Mr & Mrs A Clay
F T C Claydon
Raymond Clayton
Margaret Cochrane
T Cockcroft
Brian Cockhill
Mr M Colbeck
D M Coldwell

Lillian Josephine Coleman
Sam Collins
Tim Collins
Ivan Conroy
Elsie May Cooper
Hazel M Cooper
Mr C G Corcoran
Mr Peter Costello
R H Coward
Mrs E Craig
Stewart Crank
Mr Lawrence Crawshaw
Mr & Mrs Philip Crawshaw
Mr Robert Craven
Raymond Crockett
Mr & Mrs G Crossland
Stuart Crossland
D Crowther
David Crowther
Judith Crowther (*née* Knockton)
Mr Stanley Crowther
Mr Barry Crum
Ellen Curry
Douglas A Dagge
Susan M Daker
Rene Darby
Michael Davenport
Mrs Ripley & David
Lt. Col. D J Davies MBE
Mrs Margaret Davies
Valerie Davies
Carl Dawson
Mr P N Dawson
Mrs Winifred Day
Mr Hugh Dean
Norman Dearnley
Anthony T Denton
Geoffrey Dinkel
Brian & Christina Ditchfield
Ken & Pam Ditchfield
Terry Dobson
David R Doig
John Donnelly
Ralph Draper
Robert & Sarah Drummond
Mrs Bronwen Drury
Mr & Mrs D Duckett
J S Duckett
P Duckworth
S I Duffton
Mr C Duffy
Norman Duffy
Brenda Dunne
Raymond H Dunning
Miss Valerie Durham
Donald Ian Dyson
Frank Dyson
Mr & Mrs G Dyson
Oliver Dyson
Vilma Dyson
Mr F Earnshaw
A S Eastwood
George Eastwood
Mr D R Eaton
Mrs Mary Eccles
Mrs Maureen Eccles
Mr & Mrs D Ellam
Robert Elliott
Frank Ellis
Trevor & Colleen Ellis
Elsie M Eva
Mr Harry Thomas Evans
James Ewens
Jean Ewing
Mr William Exley
Ivor G Fallas
Dennis & Pauline Farmer
Clive Farrand
J F R Farrow
Mr B J Fawcett
Brian Field
Brian Russell Firth
George & Joan Firth

T M Foley
Kevan Ford
Garry A Foster
Mr Geoffrey Foster
Jean & Eric Foster
Peter R Foster
Willie Fox
Roger France
Donald J Free
Dorothy E Free
Lynn F Free
Richard R Free
Terry Fuller
Rosamund P Gallagher
John C Galvin
Dr John Galvin
Shirley Galvin
Sheila & Vic Gammon
Mr Thomas Gannon
Maurice Garlick
Kenneth Garside
Melvin Stuart Garside
Michael Gatenby
Christine Gee
Melvyn Gibson
David F Gledhill
E Gledhill
Keith Gledhill
Philip Gledhill
Justin Mark John Goodyear
William & Anne Gore
Donald Gothard
Donald Gothard
David Goude
Dennis Goude
Mrs Pam Graham
Stephanie Grant-Allen
Stephen Green
Muriel Greenhaigh
J R Greensnth
Mrs Margaret Gregory
Agnes Scott Grieve
Jean Hadfield
Enid & Brian Hadley
Barbara Haigh
Evelyn Haigh
Frank Haigh
Mr & Mrs Frank Haigh
John Michael Haigh
John Rowland Patrick Haigh
Josie Haigh
Phyllis Haigh
Robert A Haigh
Tony Haigh
L Haigh
Mr Karl Hales
Jean Hallas
M J Hallas
Ronald Hamer
Andrew Hampshaw
Geoffrey Hampson
Simon D Hampson
Deborah Hancock
Brian Hannam
Michael Arthur Hannam
J S Hanson
Michael Hardcastle
Florence & Trevor Hargreaves
Mrs J Harpin
P M Harris
W G Harris
Mr Brian Harrison
David Harrison
Gerry Hartley
Richard Hartley
G Hawthornthwaite
V H & Elsie Hay
Mrs Joan M Hayward
Jennifer & Malcolm Heap
Brian Hebblethwaite
Mr & Mrs J Hebblethwaite & Family
Michael B Henkel
Bernard Hepworth
David & Linda Herbert
Gerald Heywood
Geoffrey Hill
Mrs Rose Miriam Hill
David Hilton
Keith Hinchliffe
Mr J A Hinchliffe

R & M Hinchliffe
Randall Hinchliffe
Mr C Hinkley
Arthur Hirst
David Hirst
David A Hirst
Mrs E M & Mr J M Hirst
Mr John Hirst
Mrs S M Hirst
Mr Willie Hodgson
Mr Peter Holdsworth
David Lewis Hollingworth
A F Holroyd
David M Holroyd
Mr S Holroyd
John Hooley
Cynthia K Hooper
Margaret Hooper
Rita Hopping
Mr Peter Horvath
Mr S C Howard
Elizabeth Anne Howarth
B Howe
Graham Howe
Mr Walter Howson
J Malcolm Hoyle
Malcolm & Susan Hoyle
'The Do You Remember When Group' St Lukes
Hospital, Huddersfield
Matthew P Hunt
Mrs F M Hurst
Susan R Ingham
C G Irving
J A Irving
Mr G N Jacklin
Mrs E D Jackson
Kevin Stuart Jackson
PA Jackson
C M Jarratt
David Jenkins
Edward Jenkins
Brian Jenkinson
Mrs P A Jennett
David P Jepson
H Jessop
J A Jessop
P T Jessop
Ian R Jones
Jacqueline M Jones
Mrs June Jones
Mrs C & Mr C Kahayan
Mr Michael A Kay
John Kaye - Shadwell - Leeds
John A Kaye
Mrs M Kaye
Mrs Margaret Kaye
Mr Noel S Kaye
Philip Kaye
Mrs T Kaye
Mrs Winifred Kaye
Mr Martin Kaye
Sue Zabiela - Western Australia
Mary Keady
Mrs H M Keeley
Eddie Keating
Brian Kelly
Mr W J Kendall
Mr Vance Kenny
Brian Kenyon
Mr J E Kergon
Geoffrey W Kershaw
Mr B Kilner
Stanley & Irene Kilvington
Mrs Maureen Kinnear
The Beaumont Arms - Kirkstile
Mrs G Kitching
Tony Knapton
Raymond Knight
Betty & Nick Korol
Gordon J Ladell
Brian Lawton
Gilbert Lawton
Mr Adrian Lee
Mr T Lee
G A Lees
Eric & Margaret Levett
Mr David Lewis
Theresa Lightfoot
Barry Lockwood
Irene Mary Lockwood

John Lockwood
Mr J A Lockwood
Paul Lockwood
Mr Philip Lockwood
Alec Lodge
Stanley Lodge
John Longbottom
John Trevor Longbottom
Mark Andrew Longbottom
Mr A P Lonton
Kevin & Lorraine
Mary Alwyn Lover
C E Lumb
Richard George Lumb
Alan & Shirley Lunn
Robert Lunn
Macaskie
Iain MeFalls
John McHugh
Ian & Elaine McKean
Ian McKenzie
Allan McLean
Alex McNeil
Ken Makin
Brian Mallinson
Mr R Mallinson
Jim Mansfield
Vera Markey
C Marsden
Denise Caine Marshall
David Matthews
Sheila and Jack Maynard
Sephen C Measham
Esmé Mellor
James Mellor
John & Carol Mellor,
Mr Norman Mellor
Rodney Mensah
David Meredith
Hal Mettrick
B & S Midwood
Sheila Millington
Charles Buchan Milne
Mr G P Milnes
M Milnes
Mrs B Mitchell
Mr D Mitchell
Mr E Mitchell
Eric Mitchell
Peter Vaughan Mitchell
Harold R Moon
Miss Annie L Moore
George Moorhouse
K J & C Moorhouse
Ronnie Moorhouse
Roy Moorhouse
Stephen Moorhouse
Mr Stephen M Moran
Shirley Le Morellec
Miss D J Morrell
David Morrell
Mark A Morrell
Rona Mortimer
Joan & Dennis Morton (on their Ruby Wedding)
Geoffrey Mosley
John & Anne Mullany
Paul Mullany
Eamonn Murphy
Peter T Nicholas
Danny Noble
Trevor Noble
William Noble
Michael Norcliffe
Mr Alec North
Alfred North BEM
Richard Oates
Leonard Oliver
Mr E J O'Sullivan
Outlane Junior School
David J Pack
Mrs Bessie Page
Mrs Jennifer Palliser
Kenneth Palmer
Mike Parkin
Donald Parkinson
Geoffrey S Parkinson
Russell Parkinson
Selwyn Pearce
Frank Pearson
Josephine Pearson

Norma Pearson
M Peel
Susan Mary Peel
Brian Pember
Pickford Contracting
The Pickles Fanly - Kirkheaton
Mr G L Pilling
Ian A M Pogson
Mrs M Polis
Brian Polley
Mrs D G Pontefract
K Porter
Raymond P Prior
Michelle Proctor
Charles David Pugh
Harry Pugh
David Michael Pullein
A & M Quarmby
Mavis Quinn
Raymond Radford
George Ramsay
Geoff Ramsden
Mr Eric Raper
David Rawnsley
Colin & Hilary Reeves
Beverley Reoch
Harold Rhodes
Lewis Rhodes
Mrs Pamela Rhodes
Eric & Jean Richardson
Martin Richardson
Roland & Marylin Rickett
Andrea J Roberts
Carmel & Chris Roberts
Colin Hall Roberts
G Philip Roberts
Lewis Robinson
Mr Frank Rockett
Rev S W Roebuck
Wilfred O Roebuck
K T Rollinson
Clifford Rothery
David J Rothwell
Elizabeth S Sanderson (Hunt)
Brian Saville
Jane Scaramuzza
Andrew George Schofield
Mr G Schofield
Gladys & Clifford Schofield
Stuart Schofield
Hunter Scott
Margaret Scott
Betty Senior
Jack Senior
C Shackleton
David M Shackleton
John F Sharp
R F Sharpe
Jonathan P Shaw
Michael P Shaw
Mike and Shirley Shaw
Maureen Shelton (née Brook)
Mrs Shields
Corby Jayne Short
Neil Shuttleworth
Nadine & John Marshall Simmons
Sandra Simmons
Trevor Simpkins
D B Simpson
Stewart Sinclair
N D Singleton
J J & M Sloan
Brenda Smith
Mrs Ellen Celia Smith
Gordon Smith
G Raymond Smith
James Smith
Mr James Stuart Snth
Peter Smith
Philip Charles Smith
Richard Stephen Smith
Mrs S A Smith
John & Geraldine Snowball
Sam Sowerby
Mr Brian Sparkes
Colin Spivey
Mr & Mrs J Spooner
Colin Stafford
Mrs Joan L Stanford
Mark A Stannard

Gary Stead
Violet Holdsworth Bentley Stead
A M Stephenson
Arthur Stockhill
A H Stocks
Len Storey
Linda Stott
Mr & Mrs P Sunderland
E A Sutcliffe
Mrs E M Swales
Mrs W M Swallow
A Swift
George Swift
Mr C Sykes
Connie Sykes
David Keith Sykes
Edward Carl Sykes
Evelyn Sykes
Gordon Sykes - Honley
Gordon Sykes - Lepton
J A Sykes
J T & M Sykes
James Ashton Sykes
Jean Sykes
John & Bronwyn Sykes
K Sykes
M K Sykes
Stephen John Sykes
Mr S N Sykes
Winifred Petch Sykes
Mr Brian Tann
Bernard & Pat Tattersall
Brian & Ann Tattersall
Brian Taylor
Hazel Taylor
J B Taylor
James & Barbara Taylor
Jean Taylor
Kenneth Taylor
Philip Taylor
Tom Taylor
Vera Taylor
Mr D Telford
Mr Alex W Tetlaw
H Thomas
Anthony Thornton
Joan M Thornton
Andrea Thwaites
Mrs Doreen Toninson
Paul A Townend
Sam Tracey
Neil & Diane Trenberth
Raymond Tunnacliffe
G H Tunnicliffe
David Mark Turner
The Verlander Family
Colin Waddington
Mr & Mrs J D Waddington
Kenneth Edwin Wade
Malcolm H Wade
P Wade
Peter Wade
Mr & Mrs Brian D Wadsworth
Mr & Mrs D Roger Wadsworth
Mr D Wadworth
John Alan Walker
Mrs Anne Walker
D Rodney H Walker
David Ian Hardy Walker
Peter C Walker
Reg Walker
David & Daphne Wallace
Marlene Anne Walsh
Mr Granville Ward
M Ward
Barry Watkinson
Jean Weatherhead
Mrs Margaret E Welsh
Wendy
Sandra West
David Whelan
Stuart Whitaker
Barbara White
Marie Whitebread
Frank Whitehead
H D Whitehead
Leonard Whitehead
Peter Whitehouse
F Whiteley
Joyce Whiteley

Annie Whitwam
Mrs Mavis Whitwam
Philip Whitwam
Alan Whitworth
D A & V M Whitworth
Peter G Whitworth
Robin & Janet Widdup
Annette Wiley
Barbara Wilkinson
David E Wilkinson
Miss W M Wilkinson
Mr Roy Wilkinson
Mr & Mrs W E Willey
John A Williamson
Douglas Wilson
Maureen Wilson
Roy Wilson
Mrs L Wimpenny
Eric Winstanley
Mr A W Wise
Ken Wood
Kenneth Wood
Walter Wood
William Wood
Donald George Woods
William Dyson Woodward
Annie Wormald
Derek Wright
Douglas G & Gillian R Wright
Mr M Wright
Mrs Shirley Wrigley
Mr & Mrs B Wroe
Celia Wylde
Alfred Henry Yeadon